LET'S START
FLY-FISHING

Fiona Armstrong

LET'S START
FLY-FISHING
The Rules of the Game

Foreword by Bill Currie

Illustrations by Tony Pope

NEIL WILSON PUBLISHING

To my husband, Rodney Potts

Text © Fiona Armstrong, 1999
Illustrations © Tony Pope, 1999

With grateful thanks to the late Neil Graesser, OBE
for all his help and encouragement.

Neil Wilson Publishing Ltd
303a, The Pentagon Centre
36 Washington Street
GLASGOW G3 8AZ
Tel: 0141-221-1117
Fax: 0141-221-5363
E-mail: nwp@cqm.co.uk
http://www.nwp.co.uk/

A catalogue record for this book is
available from the British Library.

ISBN 1-897784-28-7

Designed by Mark Blackadder

Printed by Interprint, Malta

CONTENTS

BILL CURRIE

Foreword

It is all too easy to tell the world that fishing is a question of the fisher, the tackle and the fish. Of course this is true, but like many limited or misleading statements about fishing, it misses the point. Fishing is about passion and fun. Look even deeper and it is about fascination and compulsion and it touches on the deepest longings and the most satisfying delights available to us. Fiona's new book looks like a salmon-fishing primer, with sections on the fish, the tackle and tactics of the sport, but look deeper and you will see that it is something quite different from a how-to-do-it book. It is a *vade mecum*, literally a 'come fishing with me' book. That means that you are invited to share the author's experiences, her asides, her delight in the sport and her chuckles as she fishes.

This is a book full of places, people and atmosphere. It begins with a famous after-supper poem in broad Lowland Scots on 'the rules o' the game' – the kind of poem you want to call 'a recitation' – and it conjures up memories of a fishing club dinner with its warmth and conviviality. The book ends with character portraits of ghillies and a collection of their tales. In between, you will never be far from a telling quotation, a bit of dialogue, a vignette of a fishing character or a tale from Fiona's own experience. That means you will never be far from a laugh, a raised eyebrow or a moment of reflection.

As you read, however, you will also never be far from the essential arts of fishing. Systematically, Fiona presents a picture of the fish, where and how salmon are fished, what rods, reels and lines they require and all the apparatus of fishing. You will also be aware of prominent words set in capital letters. These are the fundamental terms of any fishing discussion – the canon of our sport – and are listed in the glossary. Do I hear you say, 'How tedious.' Look again. Between the term *Double* (hooks) and *Dropper* (flies) falls the term *Dram*. Need I say more! It is the most un-dull glossary I have ever read.

Fiona's handbook on the sport is her own unique vision of fishing, a slice of her own joy in going to the waterside, meeting other fishers and outwitting salmon. As a way to learn how to fish for salmon, it is a sound, clear-headed, up-to-date treatise and a compendium of some of the best asides and tales in the sport. This is fishing – as much about people and experiences as knowing all about rods, reels, lines and fish, as Fiona skilfully reminds us.

BILL CURRIE, LILLIESLEAF, JUNE 1999

CHAPTER ONE

The Rules o' the Game

When you're fishing for salmon,	
That is wi' the flea*	*fly
There's some things ye mauna*	*must not
And some ye maun dee.*	*must do
Be it cauld, weet or het,*	*cold, *wet or hot
Bright, lowering, or clear,	
Aye*, fish wi' the flea,	*Always
What ere ye mon* hear.	*might
There are fleas o' a' colours	
And ithers beside.	
But pey nae* attention,	*pay no
Let size be your guide.	
Gin* he rises gey* and often,	*Until, lively
But willna* tak haud,*	*will not, *hold
A smaller flea try,	
Then wait for the thud.	

When watters are big,
Fish the tail o' the stream,
Wi' a muckle* big flea   *large
And some lead.
It may spoil your casting
And will glisten maybe,
But the fish on the bottom
Will hae something tae see.
When salmon they tak,
Wi' a sworle on the tap,
Dinna* strike like at troots,*   *Don't, *trout
Or your line will gang* slack.   *go
But wait till he turns
Has the hook i' his throat.
A flick o' the tip,
Is a' that is sought.
But if it's deep doon he taks,
Wi' a thud that near shaks ye,
He's hookit* already,   *hooked
Nae more tae dae.
But up wi' the pint*   *tip
And put on the strain
Get richt up ammenst* him,   *amongst
He'll go like a train.
Now counter each move,
Wi' just enough force.
And lead him tae safety,

Like driving a horse!
For he jump, drop the pint.
Let the line gang slack
And pray he is still there and
Soon will be back.
Then up pint again
And tak up the strain
And soon in your bag,
Ye'll be takin' him hame.
Through the day noo 'n* then,   *now and
Take time tae sit doon.
Mak* sure that your line knots   *Make
And hooks are a' soon.*   *sound
Check the pint o' yore hook,
It should aye be richt sharp.
Keep a file in your bag,
It will pay for the work.
Ye think he's played oot
When he turns on his back.
But he's aye got anither
Trump caird* in the pack   *card
And just as ye slack line
And reach oot
Tae fit on the tailer
Or stick in the hook
He revives at yince,*   *once
Wi' a dive and a splash

A flick o' his tail
And he's gane* in a flash   *gone
Now if you pay attention
Tae all that I say
Sport will ensue,
Some time i' the day
But wait, haud a minit,*   *hold on a minute
Consider, think again.
Hae* the salmon been tellt*   *Has, *told
The RULES O' THE GAME?

ANON

CHAPTER TWO

The Salmon

*'The salmon is accounted the King of freshwater fish,
and is ever bred in rivers relating to the sea, yet so
high or far from it as admits no tincture
of salt or brackishness.'*

ISAAK WALTON, *THE COMPLEAT ANGLER*, 1653

I remember that spring day clearly. It was fairly typical Highland weather, slightly overcast and damp, with a hint of warmth promising better things to come. As always in Scotland, we'd breakfasted well and arrived at the river, fuelled with porridge, kippers and oatcakes and fired with enthusiasm for the coming day. And what a day! First cast for my husband and bang! There was a salmon on the end, a large, silvery, 15-lb beauty which tugged and strained at the end of his line. It danced angrily in and out of the water and my heart was in my mouth. But despite the commotion, my husband, a veteran fisher, kept his nerve.

Eventually, after what seemed like a lifetime, but was probably only 20 minutes or so, he called for the net and we landed the first fish of the year and laid it out, sparkling in the grass.

My husband had used a two-inch Waddington, a large hairy fly, so I attached the same and climbed gingerly down the bank. Two minutes later and my line tightened too as a huge spring fish came leaping out of the pool. More out of the water than in, it careered up and down and all I could hear was the splashing of the water and my husband beside me, muttering, 'I don't like it!' I didn't like it either, for suddenly the line went slack. What looked like a 17-pounder, the biggest I had ever had at the end of my line, had gone.

'What did I do wrong?' I asked in anguish.

'You should have dropped your rod-tip when it leapt out of the water. It puts less strain on the line,' was the reply. Now he tells me, I thought! However, forewarned was forearmed and the next salmon was a certainty – an 11-pounder that I placed proudly on the bank. A morning to remember for a fly-fisher, for such times are rare and magical.

There's no getting away from it. To catch a salmon is something special. Maybe it's the way they look; the rose-pink flesh clothed in silver. Or perhaps it's the fact that salmon spells 'special occasion'. Wherever it's served, at weddings, races or regattas, and however it comes, dressed in aspic, smoked, or just straight from the tin, there's always a hint of luxury. Salmon still has star-quality – and that's despite the fact that it's now readily obtainable from numerous salmon farms. We're not quite at the days of salmon and chips, but almost!

Cheap and plentiful it was too, in centuries past. Then, like the oyster, the salmon was an everyday food. In fact it was so common that estate workers had it written into their terms of employment that they wouldn't have to eat it more than twice a week. Imagine! if only today's fisher could enjoy the same condition: 'Thou shalt not catch salmon more than twice a week.' The sad fact is that although there may be plenty of farmed salmon about, the fish that we are after, the river, or WILD SALMON, seems increasingly elusive. It is definitely a case of the good old days. Talk to any seasoned angler and he'll recall times when all it took were a few, fruitful hours to catch a fish; and the further you go back, the better it appears to have been.

Take this Victorian report from a game magazine, which refers to one week's fishing on the River Eden in Cumbria.

> A salmon of 56-lb was killed here last Friday. On Wednesday, Mr E L Hough, solicitor, killed in the Crosby water nine fish, (weighing over 200 lb), and on Friday eight more. A number of fish were landed in the Linstock water. Mr H Ford Barclay of Monkhams, Essex caught

eight, the heaviest a very fine fresh-run fish of 41-lb, Mr Bland had eleven, six of which were over 20-1b. In the lower portion of Rickerby water, Mr MacInnes, MP, the proprietor, killed six fish last week, the heaviest 29-lb, Mr J. MacInnes landed five. At Eden Banks, Mr R R Hall of Liverpool has killed fifteen salmon in six days…

And so on and so on! A hundred years later and how times have changed. These days a salmon a year would be cause for much rejoicing. It could be that 20th-century fishers are less proficient than their Victorian counterparts, but I somehow doubt it. So what's happening? Why are some Highland rivers seeing their catches halved? And why has the world catch of salmon fallen alarmingly over the last few decades?

There are so many reasons. Pollution; large-scale fishing at Atlantic feeding grounds; over-enthusiastic commercial netting at river mouths; drift netting; poaching; anglers who take too many fish; the introduction of foreign species of fish which upsets the ecological balance; disease like infectious salmon anaemia; commercial salmon farms with their infestations of sea-lice and acid rain. All of these affect the wellbeing of the salmon. Even the innocent-looking grey seal, which is increasing in number around our coastline, stands accused of greedily working his way through precious stocks.

Several decades ago, game fishing was enjoying a boom, with new, exciting methods of fishing and revolu-

tionary types of tackle coming onto the market. As we look at the next century, the future is not quite so hopeful. Such is the concern over the decline, that many places now rightly have limits on the number of salmon that rod-fishers can take. Some go further and insist that all caught fish are returned. Until we can find some way of reversing the trend, both the above measures may be the way ahead if we are to continue to try to catch the king of fish.

You can do your bit, though. Join a fisheries protection group like the Salmon and Trout Association, which has the salmon's best interests at heart.

But let's look at the life of this magnificent creature. A salmon comes into the world as a tiny egg laid in the gravel of a stream or river. As a baby, it's called a FRY, but by the end of a year, it's become what's known as a PARR. It's now a little fish of between three and five inches (7.5-12.5cm) which feeds on insects and worms and survives by avoiding predators like birds and bigger fish. When it takes on a silver colour, it's known as a SMOLT and is ready to migrate to the sea. If it stayed, it wouldn't survive. Few rivers could provide enough food for thousands of full-grown salmon, and so the smolts, in their thousands, head for the salt water and the rich feeding grounds of the ocean.

Here, in this new kingdom, they eat voraciously, feeding on smaller fish and plankton. Such is their appetite that, by the end of the first year, the smolts that left the rivers can be 20 times their original size. But although a salmon matures at sea, it cannot spawn there; this can only be done in fresh water and at some stage it must come home. Not to any old home, though, for a salmon will head for the self-same river in which it was spawned and to almost the same spot. This returning to spawn is called a RUN and some rivers have a SPRING RUN and others an AUTUMN one. Indeed, some have a run all year round, but whenever a salmon comes back, it must wait for late autumn or winter before it lays its eggs.

So they return. Swimming with great determination through the sea at speed, they have one purpose: to find their native water. How they manage to work their way around continents and across oceans remains one of nature's great mysteries, but some scientists think their sense of direction is connected to magnetic centres in the brain. Another theory is that salmon have a good sense of smell and are guided in by the distinctive scent of their own river estuary. Whatever brings them back, following finely-tuned instincts and surviving hazards like the seal and the fisherman's net, they reach the mouth of their home river and here the last stretch begins.

Upstream they go, racing along, for these fish have amazing stamina. Their great tails and fins are well-developed by strenuous exercise at sea and it's this strength which allows them to tackle the most daunting obstacles. Swimming with great determination against the current, they carefully avoid lurking nets, they resist lures and negotiate rocky pools and waterfalls. Salmon are incredible jumpers and their Latin name suits them well. *Salmo Salar. Salar* means The Leaper.

Nowhere is this more clearly demonstrated than on the falls of the Rivers Cassley and Shin in Sutherland, which stretch up in stages 50-feet (15m) and more. Out of the still water, the fish enter the roaring foam and then hurl themselves towards a platform several feet up, before being washed back into the pool. Nothing daunted, they valiantly regroup, some trying for days, even weeks, in their quest to reach the spawning grounds several miles up the glen. Here, jumps of six or seven feet (2m), are quite common, but the highest leap for a salmon, recorded in Scotland, is 12 feet (3.8m). How they manage to propel themselves upwards with such amazing force is a modern-day mystery, although, in 1653, the father of fishers, Isaak Walton, maintained they did it by putting their tails in their mouths and catapulting themselves up!

The most determined eventually reach their destination and it is here, in the gravelly spawning grounds, that the hard work pays off. During their life at sea, salmon tend to swim in shoals, but on entering the freshwater, the male COCK fish will pair up with a female HEN fish. In the shallow water, the hen digs a hole in the river bed into which she deposits her eggs, which are in turn fertilised by the cock. But for most of them, that is

sadly the end; after spawning, around 75% of salmon will die and only a handful remain to return to the sea. Emaciated and exhausted, these hardy survivors make their way downstream and the life-cycle starts again.

Those which do survive are known as KELTS and if you catch one, which is easily done as they come downstream in early spring, the rules say you must return it to the water at once. It can't be eaten, so you may as well be magnanimous. But putting a kelt back is one thing, recognising one is not quite so easy. The textbook definition is a 'thin, blackened, often diseased fish'. But a kelt can also be well-mended, that is, by the time it's caught, it may have regained some of its original silver colour and put on some weight. In short, it can be difficult to distinguish a kelt from a fresh salmon, especially for the inexperienced.

As a rough rule, expect to catch kelts in early spring. Be suspicious when a fish half-heartedly takes the fly and then proceeds to flop about in the water. It may feel like you've hooked a piece of floating wood and it may not look that thin and black. Check the gills: if there are maggots nestling there, it's a sure sign. Put it back to live another day and, with luck, another season. It may return to the sea to fatten again and come back next season as a healthy, silvery fish.

It is a difficult area, for the question of a kelt can be an emotive issue. Is it, or is it? Sometimes it is only apparent when the angler cuts it open on the kitchen table and finds the flesh, grey, dry and unappetising. The advice is, if uncertain, put it back. One thing's for sure, if you doubt your own fish, so will everyone else. It's a heartbreaking decision, I know, especially if it's your first salmon, but, believe me, you'll feel infinitely worse if you kill it, only to find it's inedible. Meanwhile if you want to avoid having to make that vital judgement, then fish in summer and autumn, as it's generally agreed that by May, most kelts will have reached the sea and be well out of harm's way.

But it's not all bad news, as we find with the GRILSE. A grilse is a young salmon which has returned to spawn after one sea winter. It may weigh only a few pounds, but if you catch one covered in sea lice, it means that it's just come into the fresh river water from the sea and it will be delicious. Note here: do not confuse sea lice with maggots: sea lice found on the backs of silvery salmon are a sign of freshness. Maggots in the gills are a sign of decay.

And that, briefly, is the salmon. A fish that can range from a few pounds in weight up to the largest ever caught in British waters on rod and line. It was hooked by Miss Georgina Ballantine, back in 1922, on the Tay in Perthshire and it weighed a staggering 64 lbs. The record for a salmon caught on the fly is 61 lbs and that was taken on the Deveron by Clementina Morrison. Women do catch the biggest fish, but that's another story; it's either to do with their hormones, or their innate skill, depending on whom you believe.

There are so many tales and theories about the salmon, for it's a fish that has been studied by naturalists and anglers for centuries and still remains a source of mystery. For example, why is it that when a salmon comes back to the river to spawn, it doesn't actually feed in the river? How does it survive? The answer is by stocking up at sea and eating enough food to last it the many months it will need to work its way up-river. It's an amazing fact, when you consider the distance a salmon has to travel and the amount of energy it uses in battling its way upstream.

It must be nature's way of protecting the species. Just imagine if hundreds of 20-lb salmon were inclined to feed as voraciously in a river as they did in the ocean. Because of the sheer size and numbers, they would soon clean out the pools and jeopardise the survival of their own species.

But if a salmon doesn't look for food in a river, why does it go for the fisherman's fly? Well, there are various explanations, some more romantic than others. Some say the salmon is a bad-tempered creature who snaps irritably at anything dangled before him; others claim it takes the lure out of habit, the feathered freshwater morsel stirring some faint memory of a tasty titbit from the sea.

Indeed, there are all sorts of theories in salmon-fishing and some are fairly comprehensible and straight-forward. But it's always the same; you make a certain statement about this king of fish and he does something completely different. In fact, it's an unpredictable sport all round and there's never a right way or a definite reason for anything. And just when you think you've found one, something happens to confound it. I'm afraid that when it comes to catching a salmon, as in the *Fisher's Lament* it's simply a case of yesterday, tomorrow, next week... Alas, never today!

> *Sometimes ower early, sometimes ower late.*
> *Sometimes nae water, sometimes a spate,*
> *Sometimes ower calm, sometimes ower clear.*
> *There's aye something wrang, when I'm fishing here!*

CHAPTER THREE

Learning to Fish

Angling may be said to be so like the mathematics,
that it can never be fully learnt.

ISAAK WALTON, *THE COMPLEAT ANGLER*, 1653

Yes, you *are* allowed to fish for salmon. You don't have to be titled or rich, although that can help – as can experience. Meet veteran anglers who've been fishing for 50 years, and they may tell you they know 'a little bit' about the subject. They're not being modest; you see, there's so much to see and do in fly-fishing – and just when you think you're getting on top of it, something happens to change it all. Then, of course, it dawns that the only true experts are the fish.

But don't let this be a discouragement. The fact that it's so varied and unpredictable is also the beauty of the sport. From that first, fearful cast with a long salmon rod, through the frustration of flogging away for hours on the river, to the glimmer of hope when you spot a large fin in a corner of the pool, to the gritty determination to make something of the day and finally to that huge surge of excitement as you reel in a gleaming salmon.

So how do you learn to fish for salmon? Well, basically, you've got to get someone to teach you, but not a husband or wife. Would you let them teach you to drive? No, for the sake of good marital relations, choose anyone but a better half. Consider this conversation between two newly-weds overheard on the banks of the River Dee.

'Well, here we are, my love. I promise you'll pick it up in no time. In fact, we'll soon have it cracked.'

(How right he was. Cracked on the ear, cracked on the nose, cracked on the back of the head. Even without a fly at the end, 25 metres of plastic-coated line can still deliver a hefty whack to whichever part of the anatomy gets in the way. Half-an-hour into the proceedings and his patience is wearing thin.)

'Darling, I've told you. Don't throw it, flick it. Just let the rod do the work!'

'Sweetie, I've told you, I'm not throwing it.'

'Darling, I'm afraid you are. Oh, for God's sake, just watch where you're putting that thing! [He rubs the red welt on the side of his face] Look, it's so simple – a child could do this. Watch me again.'

'A child could do this? No, I don't want to watch you again. I'm doing quite well on my own, thank you!'

'OK, if you're so good at it – you carry on! I'm going down river to do some fishing myself.'

And off he goes in a sulk. And there she is, with a 13-foot salmon rod in her hands – small by fly-fishing standards but enormous to a novice – and an increasing desperation to get wildly flailing line and lure under control. Defiantly she ties on a fly which starts to live up to its name. Flying up trees, into banks and across her nose. And then, it actually lands where it's supposed to...on the water. A half-reasonable cast and bang! The reel jerks into life. And now we have another story: she has caught a fish and he has not. Is that, I ask, good grounds for a happy marriage?

No, choose a friend, an uncle, even a long-lost cousin. All of these will do fine and should prove a cheap and cheerful way of learning, your only outgoings being the odd bottle of whisky. But if you don't know anyone who fishes, you must be prepared to invest some cash and either take PROFESSIONAL INSTRUCTION or join a FISHING CLUB.

Go out and buy a reputable fly-fishing magazine. Look for one with the word 'salmon' in the title and you won't go far wrong. Now, leaf through to the back, taking in the wonderful glossy pictures of rivers and fish, and here in the end pages, will be adverts for fly-fishing courses. If the teacher has an advanced Professional Game Angling Instructor's qualification (APGAI) or a Salmon

and Trout Association National Instructor's Certificate
(STANIC), all the better. Please note here, even if learning
from a friend, do try to get some professional lessons as
well, because it's rather like learning to drive a car or swing
a golf club. Start correctly and you shouldn't pick up too
many bad habits.

The thing is, when observing as a beginner, it all looks
so easy. Just throw back the line, cast away and Bob's your
uncle! Or is he? It's only when you actually hold that
fishing rod that the truth about timing and handling
begins to dawn. In fact, teaching the novice to fish must be
a nightmare. For a start, the instructor runs the certain risk
of being scarred for life, after being hit by flailing line and
fly. And even if he or she has got nerves of steel, unless
they've also got bags of patience, they'll soon get fed-up
with repeating perfectly simple instructions like, 'Up...
back, pause...forward, and let go!' (The line that is, not the
rod as well...) On the other hand, the long-suffering
teacher may get a real know-all, someone who catches a
fish on the second cast of the day.

Connecting with a fish on your first trip to the water
is what's known as BEGINNER'S LUCK. Happily, this
seems to occur rather a lot. But, why should this be?
Perhaps it's the technique. For, unlike the smooth casts of
an experienced fisher, the novice will be highly unpredictable. Their movements will be erratic, with the line
going here, there and everywhere and it's this jerkiness that

may tantalise or irritate the fish into snapping at the fly. Or it may be that they catch something because they are doing things more carefully and methodically. For example, they may be wading slowly and therefore covering the water more thoroughly. Whatever the theory, a newcomer definitely has a sporting chance of coming up trumps.

There are exceptions to the rule, though, and despite their best efforts, some folk never catch anything. If you're consistently drawing a blank, you become despondent. Some anglers go a step further. Not only do they not catch anything, they also jinx the whole fishing party, so that no-one catches anything. Feel very sorry for these people, but do not include them in your plans. Empty hours spent on river banks can fuel the fires of superstition. So be wary when you meet people who have fished for 20 years and never caught a salmon. It's either dedication beyond the call of duty, madness or worse – and it's certainly one in the eye for beginner's luck!

But, whenever and however you land your first salmon, it will be a day to remember. Whatever it looks like and whatever it tastes like, it will be your first and you will dine out on the story for years to come. It is only when looking back in saner moments that you will quietly admit that it was a bit of a dog. At the time, it might be the oldest, blackest fish in the river. To you, it will seem like an oil painting.

Your first salmon! It is something to always

remember. The amazement, as you realise there's something at the end of the line; the panic, as you try to bring it under control; the interminable wait for the net; the careful landing – and then the incredulous look as you see it there in the net. You have caught a salmon! And of course, there'll be great rejoicing that night – probably in a bar somewhere – as the tale is told and retold, the fish getting bigger with each telling.

A salmon in the net. That is the aim. But don't be too impatient. Remember you have 50 years of 'knowing a little bit' before you. Which takes us back to Isaak Walton and his view that it can never be fully learned. But we have to start somewhere, so, take a leaf out of *Mrs Beeton's Cookbook* – 'First catch your salmon!'

CHAPTER FOUR

Where and When to Fish

'I went on this holiday and I only caught one fish.
So if you work it out, this salmon cost me £500.'

1st FISHER

'Well, if it cost you that for one, it's a good thing
you didn't catch two.'

2nd FISHER

If you want to take up fly-fishing for salmon, you may be under the delusion that all you have to do is find some water and get cracking. Well, I'm afraid you'd be wrong. Like everything else in life, angling has its rules and regulations. So let's establish a few facts. Basically, all fishing for salmon in the UK is privately owned. That water will belong to someone, either to an individual, a fishing association, a local authority, or the Crown. The angler can fish for salmon in RIVERS, RIVER ESTUARIES and LOCHS, and can do it either from the bank, by wading or from a small boat. But wherever the fisher wants to cast a line, permission will be needed and, usually, paid for. However, you'll get more than just some time on the water for your outlay: as you pay, so the owner has to look after the water. He must maintain spawning grounds and repair and improve POOLS where fish lie and BANKS where fishers stand to make it as comfortable and rewarding an experience as possible. Otherwise, the fish won't be there and you won't pay to come back.

And just as you can't fish where you want, you can't fish when you want. There is a SEASON, which varies from river to river, but it generally lasts from spring to autumn. For instance, the season on the River Earn in Perthshire starts on 1 February and ends on 31 October whereas the season on the River Usk in Wales starts in March. The remaining time is known as the CLOSE SEASON and that covers the spawning period when salmon lay their eggs. In England and Wales, anglers can fish for salmon on every day of the week, but in Scotland, fishing for salmon isn't allowed on a Sunday.

Fishing out of season, without permission, or with illegal methods, is called POACHING. A couple of centuries ago, culprits would have had their hands chopped off for their labours. Today, retribution is more likely to be a fine of several hundred pounds. But it's also

extremely embarrassing to be marched off the water after being discovered by an irate bailiff. To be honest, every angler will probably fish at some stage where he or she shouldn't, although they would never dream of being referred to as a poacher. It is almost always an innocent mistake, with a wee wander off the allotted patch. As long as it's a one-off situation, folk will forgive such a minor lapse. It's when you look at the extent of serious criminal poaching, that you understand why there is so much concern.

Gone are the times when the local fished one for the pot. Poaching is now big business and a problem that affects not just water owners, but ultimately, all anglers. It's impossible to tell how many salmon are taken illegally each

'Fish, what fish?'

year, but it's estimated to be a significant proportion of stocks. Some are netted out individually at night, others involve teams of organised gangs who can clear whole pools by emptying a substance into the water that removes the oxygen. Then all they have to do is wait for the fish to suffocate and rise to the surface. But that's only the start of the problem: as the poison kills not just the salmon, it also leaves the pool dead for months to come. And as poachers are ruthless in the way they kill fish, so they can be merciless with anyone who gets in their way. One solitary watchman is little match for a determined gang. The water watcher's job is a lonely and often impossible one, trying to patrol a stretch of river several miles long.

So, who looks after what? Well, rivers in England and Wales are monitored by a body called the Environment Agency (EA). In Scotland, waters are watched over by SEPA, the Scottish Environment Protection Agency. Some waters are completely off bounds. For example, certain spawning grounds may not be fished at all.

To sum up. Cast a line for salmon in any part of the UK and you'll need permission. That can be verbally, or in the form of a written permit. On top of a PERMIT, any angler over 12 who fishes for salmon in England and Wales will also need a ROD LICENCE. Currently these cost £57 for the year and £5.50 for a day. You can get a licence from post offices, or ring the EA on 0870 166-2662. Keep it handy when fishing, as the water watcher may ask to see it

and he's unlikely to be impressed if you can't produce it. He has the power to fine you as well if he's feeling that way. If you don't want to buy a rod licence, then fish in Scotland, where they're not required.

But enough of the paperwork. One day you may hear someonein the wokplace say in a loud voice. 'Oh, I'm just off to my beat on the Dee.' This is not some sort of upper-class fetish. Let me explain. Most rivers are divided into stretches of water called BEATS.

A big river, like the Dee, may boast up to 50 separate beats, whereas a smaller one might just have two. The number of beats doesn't necessarily denote its value, but the fact that someone's taken the time to divide it up in this way must mean it's worth taking a look at. A beat can be rented for a day, a week, or even longer. If it's a DOUBLE BANK beat, you can fish both sides of the river. If it's SINGLE BANK fishing, then it's just the one.

Now, a beat is either fished privately, or it can be let to anglers who are known as TENANTS. As a beginner, don't even consider renting until you find your feet, or in this case your waders. What the trainee angler should be doing is cultivating fishing friends – and these should preferably be very rich and very busy, because that means they'll have lots of fishing booked and very little time to actually do it, so they'll need some help to make sure it's not wasted.

It goes like this. You know a man who has a week on a two-rod beat. Now he obviously can't fish more than one rod at a time, so he may invite you to fish the other. As a novice, you should take unashamed advantage of any offer like this; in fact, you must positively jump at the chance. Just remember to arrive with a bottle of something strong and don't forget to fish hard! There's nothing worse than inviting someone who just potters about on the bank looking at the flora and fauna. If you catch a fish, you will also be expected to offer it to your host, as it is his fishing. It may stick in the throat, especially if it is your first salmon, but any gentleman would refuse it and allow you your catch. On the other hand, if he has had a blank week, he might just take it. If he does, grit your teeth, smile nicely and when you get home, write a letter of thanks.

But, as time goes by, you'll need to return favour for favour and bottles of Scotch malt and heartfelt thanks will simply not be enough. No, if you regularly accept fishing from someone, sooner or later, you will have to reciprocate and that will mean finding some of your own. He may decline your offer to come and join you on the River No Hope, but at least you'll have made the gesture.

So what's available? Well, for the well-heeled there is always the possibility of purchasing a small ESTATE: the big house with a couple of hundred acres and a salmon river running through the middle. A couple of million quid should do the job, so hang around game fairs and you just might meet a girl or boy with a rich dad. If you're already married, try the lottery!

Failing these options, the next step could be a FISHING TIMESHARE. This is where you buy some time each year on a particular river. It could be for 30 years or even for life. It will cost thousands of pounds rather than millions, but the theory is that, like a fine painting, it will prove to be an investment. There are drawbacks, however. Do you really want to fish the same beat for the next 30 years? It's also difficult to predict how waters will fare in the future. A place that fishes well now might prove disappointing ten years down the line, as the river changes, or stocks dwindle and pools silt up. On the other hand, it may improve!

But let's look at more affordable types of fishing. Beats are generally priced according to the number of salmon caught there, known as the RETURNS. To fish a top Scottish river, where they take out several thousand fish a year, could cost £200 a day for a rod. To cast out on a smaller, spate river which yields just 50 fish, may only set you back £10. And just as returns affect the price in angling, so do NAMES. Take the famous Junction Pool on the River Tweed at Kelso. Anglers would give an arm and a leg to cast one single solitary fly on its hallowed waters, but it will cost them thousands of pounds to do so.

And prices also vary according to the TIME OF YEAR. For example, there are some rivers that can be fished most of the year during the rod season. But others are really only worth bothering with at certain times. Some fish well in the spring; that is, they have a SPRING RUN. Others are better fished in the autumn and have BACK-END RUN. Check whether your chosen water has a good time. Check also whether there are rules about the amount of fish you can take. Such is the concern over falling numbers, that some rivers rightly only let anglers take one salmon. It might be a case of keeping the first fish, but putting back the second. A bit heartbreaking when your first weighs four pounds and your second a hefty 34! On other rivers, it's all CATCH AND RELEASE, particularly in the spring. On these waters, they will probably insist you fish with hooks that don't have barbs.

Most people aren't in a position to be able to waste money on hopeless fishing, so it pays to shop around. Ask other anglers if they know of anything reasonable, or scan the adverts in a reputable magazine. Bargains can be found. You may approach a river owner, do a deal and take a rod for one day a week throughout the season for £100. Or you may find a place that lets you fish for just a few pounds for the day. It has to be said, however, that unless you're very lucky, you generally get what you pay for. If offered a £10 beat on a big, prestigious river like the Tweed, it'll mean it's the wrong time of year and there isn't a cat's chance in hell of getting a fish. But never turn your nose up at it: the day can be used to perfect your Spey casting and should you, by some miracle, actually hook and land a salmon, the owners will be so amazed by your prowess, they'll probably invite you back to fish at a better time. (People like to have folk catching fish on their water, it makes the beat look fruitful.)

Another good alternative can be to book an ANGLING HOLIDAY, where fishing and hotel come as a package. You'll fish to your heart's content and be safe in the knowledge that when you start your tale of woe about the one that got away, there'll be no shortage of sympathetic ears.

But, one of the best ways a beginner can learn, is to join a local fly-fishing CLUB. These associations often have access to some of the finest fishing around, though you may have to find yourself an address in the area to qualify for membership. So, do look up long-lost great aunt Maud who just happens to live near the river in question; around £50 a year could let you on to some lovely banks and pools. The other benefit is that there will be lots of keen fishers around to show you the ropes. And these people *are* the real fishers, not the folk who do it twice a year at an expensive river in the Highlands, but the men and women who are out almost every day in the season.

Assuming you do get your salmon, there will, of course, be much celebration, but try to keep it a dignified affair. Whooping for joy is probably permitted with your first. After that, remember that the angler is not there simply to catch fish. Like Renaissance man, he embraces the completeness of the sport: communing with nature, fresh air, the water, exercise and wellbeing.

Above all, abide by the rules. If it's a gentleman's agreement that a place is fly-fishing only, then to use any other sort of bait, wooden or worm-like, is just not on. It's the most wonderful thing to catch a salmon, but always tell yourself there's more to fishing than that. One day, you may believe it!

Take heed of the story of the angler who died and went to heaven. Well, it must have been heaven, for the day was mild, there was a magnificent river and on the bank, a rather smart fly-rod. So in he waded and set to work. On his first cast there was a fish on the end of the line. He couldn't believe it! He reeled in and the salmon came willingly to the net. Then he cast out again and, yes! Another fish. He reeled in again and claimed his prize. And the next and the next! It seemed he just couldn't miss as each throw of the line produced a silvery offering. Half-an-hour later, with 20 fish on the bank, it suddenly dawned on him that he was bored. The challenge had gone. The excitement just wasn't there. And in that moment, he realised to his horror that he wasn't in heaven – and if he wasn't in heaven, there was only one other place he could be!

CHAPTER FIVE
Tackle

*'A stick and a string with a fly at one end
and a fool at the other.'*
GEORGE BERNARD SHAW

So, you still want to take up fly-fishing? Well, first of all, don't rush out and buy all the gear. Fishing TACKLE, as it's called, isn't cheap. And let's face it, until you've tried it, you won't know if you'll like it. Besides which, there are lots of weird and wonderful angling terms to get to grips with; and until you know a sinker from a floater or a Garry Dog from a Hairy Mary, sorting out what's important and what isn't can be very confusing.

If booked into a reputable fishing school, they'll almost certainly provide the basic equipment. If being taught by friends, then do try to borrow for the first few trips to the river. It shouldn't be an impossible request. Fishers are great hoarders, with usually twice as much tackle as they need. But you cannot borrow forever. So,

when you, too, are hooked, that is the time to visit the sporting or TACKLE SHOP.

I have to warn that even for a much practised shopper, this can be a daunting experience. You must have passed by these shops at some time, their windows draped with nets and green rubber, their counters covered in gaudy, mean-looking hooks, their shelves stacked with what looks suspiciously like bales of washing line. When you are introduced to the delights of angling, all will become clear. From the smartest London tackle shop, with the latest, lightest, pricey net, to the smallest Highland hut, where a ghillie's wife runs up home-made flies at a pound a time, a fascinating world of rods, reels, wellies and waders will open up. Just beware. Fishing tackle is more often than not sold alongside shooting gear, so don't let all the hardware put you off.

Hardware aside, there's no doubt that browsing in a tackle shop is a delightful pastime. The only drawback is, there's a great temptation to spend. So take your time – or better still, take an angling friend along to advise you and before getting carried away, don't forget that it's FLY-FISHING stuff you're after. Tackle for any other sort of angling is quite unsuitable. If in doubt, ask the assistant, for there should be no shortage of help in a tackle shop. Most of the folk behind the counter are fishers themselves and can advise on the type of equipment, as well as passing on fascinating gossip, like the height of local rivers and the number of salmon being caught.

So, first get your ROD. Again, make sure it's the right one: a FLY-ROD. A rod for sea-fishing or for spinning is no good to someone who wants to catch a salmon on the fly. Beginners will be relieved to know that ONE rod will do, although as they improve, they may buy another, perhaps something heavier for winter and early spring, or a lighter one for the summer. If they can afford it, that is, because rods aren't cheap.

True, you might get one for £50, but on the other hand, people have been known to pay £500 or more for something really fancy. As a beginner, you should have neither the budget nor the inclination to pay such a sum for a rod. So, just buy the best you can afford, not least because it would be awful if it snapped the first time it was used. And if you're really in need of a bargain, ask the shop if they sell second-hand equipment. But, as they say, buyer beware!

So let me tell you something about the rod. Basically, most salmon fly-rods are DOUBLE-HANDED, which means you use both hands when fishing. (Compare that to a trout rod which is a SINGLED-HANDED rod.) Salmon fly-rods vary in length, from 11 feet 6 inches upwards, although the average size seems to be around 14 to 15 feet. Happily, rods have not yet gone metric , so a 15-foot rod is simply referred to as a '15 foot' or 'footer'. So that it can be easily carried and stored, the fly-rod comes in several parts, usually three. To protect these parts, they are kept in a

covering called a SLEEVE. A sleeve can be made of canvas, plastic, leather, or even metal. Obviously, the more rigid the sleeve, the more protection there is for the rod.

Yes, today's fly-fisher has an easy life when it comes to tackle, for in times past, a day by the river would really sort out the men from the boys. Stiff, heavy salmon rods of split cane were real backbreakers, instruments of torture, which needed a man and a boy to carry them to the water and an even sturdier soul to fish them. You may like to try one of these antiquities – and they are glorious to look at and hold, but, please, magnificent though they may be, do not consider learning on your grandfather's old rod. It will put you off for life. Its place is hanging on a wall as a wonderful curiosity.

You need something lightweight, flexible and strong and there's certainly no shortage of choice. Modern rods made from carbon fibre and fibreglass mean they're easy to handle, but tough enough to take the strain of an energetic salmon. Just be careful with the really light ones, which if dropped from a height, or knocked against something hard, can easily shatter.

As for size, salmon fly-rods come in all sorts of lengths, the theory being that the longer the rod is, the greater the distance you can throw the line. You could, if you wanted, buy a 20-footer, but a novice will want something more modest. Anything from 12 feet 6 inches to 15 feet. Basically, if you are small in stature, get a smaller rod. If you are six feet tall, get something longer.

As for the make, well, there are literally hundreds of names on the market, and you'll probably end up getting quite confused, so try out a couple before buying. Get the feel of it and see whether you prefer the rod to give a little, or if you are more comfortable with something stiffer. There are some classic names on the market and if you have the money, why not splash out? There are also some excellent lesser-known brands as well. And if you are sneered at on a fancy river because you have the words 'Japanese Fish X-Citer' on the side of the rod, instead of a famous brand, then that is not the sort of place you want to be fishing anyway. (Of course you could stay and catch a fish on the offending instrument and teach them all a lesson!)

So you've chosen your rod and now you'll need a REEL. The reel is a vital piece of tackle because it controls and holds the line. Remember, you want a FLY-REEL, not a spinning-reel or any other type. Go for the best, one with a good drag, as it will last for years, if not a lifetime. Most fly-fishers end up with a couple of reels to hold different types of line and also to have as a spare. But, a cheaper alternative is to buy only one reel and several interchangeable SPOOLS – the spool being the bit in the middle of the reel that holds the line and backing.

However many spools or reels are bought, the advice from the experts is that the reel must always be in balance

with the rod. Time and time again, you'll hear that BALANCE is half the battle in good casting and really, it makes sense. Using a small, modern reel on a heavy rod, would be daft. Likewise, a lightweight rod would be next to useless weighed down by a large, metal reel. So make sure it's the correct one and also that it fits the REEL-SEAT. The tackle shop assistant should keep you right on this.

Next, you need some LINE to put on the reel. Line is basically a long length of plastic-coated thread. It's quite expensive, but experts will tell you to spend that little bit extra on getting a good quality one. And again, when buying line, think of balance. Line comes in different WEIGHTS and it's important to get the right weight. Most salmon fishing requires a line weight of 9-11, but if you look just above the butt of the rod handle, there should be a number which states the recommended weight. If in doubt, ask the shop assistant.

And as line comes in different weights, it also comes in different TYPES. And here you must decide what sort of fishing you plan to do. Anglers out in early spring when rivers are high and cold often use what's called a SINKING LINE. That is, it sinks into the water to take the fly down to the fish. But if it's late spring or summer, when temperatures are rising and rivers are low, fishers may put on a FLOATING line which floats on the surface of the water. There are other sorts of line, such as the INTERMEDIATE and the SINK-TIP and it's often difficult and confusing to

know which one to use, so let's make it simple and say a beginner will generally learn to fish with a floating line. It's so much easier to pull a long length of wet plastic from the surface of a pool than it is from the bottom.

So, you now have 25 metres of line which might seem more than enough to deal with a fish of any size. However, imagine when a 20-lb salmon snatches the fly and goes tearing down the river at a rate of knots. That is, it decides to RUN. The line will rapidly spool off the reel and be gone in no time. Whoops! Lost fish. But not if you have plenty of BACKING on your reel. Backing is thin, plaited nylon, which goes onto the reel before the line. It gives an extra 50 to 100 metres. Since a spool of backing costs just a few pounds, it's an effective and cheap means of lengthening the line.

The next piece of casting equipment is NYLON. Nylon is the link between the line and the fly. Sometimes it's called a CAST or a LEADER. Nylon carries the fly out into the water. It's supposed to be almost invisible, though whether the salmon is that easily duped, I'm not so sure!

Again, there are different breaking strains of nylon, and the right one is crucial. If it's too light, it won't take a fly out properly or, worse still, it could snap under the strain of a big fish. Likewise, if it's too heavy, it may not allow the fly to swim properly in the water. So how does a fisher know what weight to use? Well, very simply, he should gauge the strength of nylon by the river conditions

and by the size of fish he hopes to catch.

If it's early spring and you're using large flies in deep water, a stiff, strong nylon is needed to carry the heavy fly through the wind. So a breaking strain of 20lbs may be used. As the year goes on, it's possible to come down in size and in late summer, when fishing low water with tiny flies, you could go as light as 8lbs, but don't forget that on days like this, the angler always runs the risk of the nylon being broken, either by a heavy fish, or a jagged rock.

Nylon is a slippery customer. When you have cut off the length you need, put a rubber band round the remainder, to stop it from sliding off the spool. It's not expensive, costing just a few pounds a spool and unless you're particularly heavy-handed, one spool should last the season. The alternative is to buy a ready-made nylon cast, but these are pricey. A note here: these casts sometimes have what's known as a DROPPER hanging from them and this is simply another piece of nylon attached to the main piece which allows you to fish two flies in one pool: it can mean a lot of fun – and sometimes a lot of fish. But a dropper is not for beginners, because it can wind itself round the rod and bring all sorts of trouble. As a novice, you'll have enough problems dealing with one fly flapping about, let alone two!

And so to the FLY. No, the game fisher does not have to go round in search of juicy bluebottles to attach to the end of his line. Basically, salmon flies are artificial lures, hairy hooks, often brightly coloured, which float on, or merge with the water, to attract the fish. For me – and perhaps for you – this will be one of the best bits of all. Studying the hundreds of shapes, sizes and colours; choosing from delightful names like the Willie Gunn, the Collie Dog and the Tadpole; or the more graphic labels like the Munro Killer, the General Practitioner and the beginner's favourite, the Muddler.

Fashioned out of feather, silk and hair, they are tied around barbed hooks, and come in all shades – red, yellow, blue, green and black, with hints of silver tinsel across the body. Some are two inches long and brass-weighted; others are a quarter that size and as light as a real fly. There are boxes and boxes of different patterns to get lost in and every fisher ends up with hundreds. Perhaps you will even end up tying your own and become an ace FLY-TYER and you can then name your own particular fly and build up your collection. But how will you know which one to use?

Very simply, the size of the fly depends on the temperature of the water. When the water's high, cold and coloured, big flies of two inches or more will be needed. When summer comes and the water is lower and clearer, it's possible to go down to lightweight flies of half an inch or less. Then there are different types of fly. The SINGLE HOOKED FLY, with one hook, the DOUBLE, with two and the TREBLE, with three. And there's what's known as the TUBE fly, where the body of the fly can be separated

from the hook. Or the WADDINDTON. All of these are used in salmon-fishing and the angler will need to take advice as to which size and hook is best for the water and the weather. At the end of each hook may be a BARB, a jagged bit of metal designed to make it harder for the fish to get off the hook. These days, more and more anglers are fishing BARBLESS. Some say it's more of a challenge; others that they don't want to harm the fish because they are catching and releasing.

As far as colour and pattern of fly go, frankly, it doesn't matter. There are so many different types that you're as well choosing something you like the look of. As long as the SIZE is right, there's probably as good a chance of catching a fish on a yellow and silver, as there is on a blue and white. Some fishers say, 'a bright fly for a bright day, a dull fly for a dull day', so you could try that. Or you could simply follow fisher and author, Dr Malcolm Greenhalgh's advice and have a 'What Is It?' fly in your collection. You may not know the name, but as long as it's the correct size, it may hook a fish.

Moving onto other accessories. Flies will need to be kept in a FLY-BOX. Left loose at the bottom of a tackle bag, they'll get jumbled up with the nylon and you'll cut your hand on a barb when rummaging inside. Something plastic or metal will do fine, lined with foam so that you can stick the hooks into it. A wooden one has the added benefit of floating, should you happen to drop it in the water.

To carry everything but the rod, you'll need a TACKLE BAG. This can be made of anything sturdy that can stand to the odd run-in with water: a wicker fishing basket, or a canvas hold-all will do. Really, it's whatever makes you happy. Just make sure it's fairly plain. You don't want to spend precious time disentangling line from numerous hooks and straps.

And when the fish is hooked, you'll need a SALMON NET. Try to get a good one, as a net can take a lot of punishment. It might get caught on spiky bushes and knocked on rocks and it needs to stand the test of time. It may also be called upon to act as an impromptu wading stick, so make sure it's strong. Remember that salmon nets tend to be large and unwieldy, so anglers with small cars may like to consider a collapsible one. Just make sure it's put up correctly, so it doesn't collapse at the wrong time – that is, just when you're about to net a fish.

You may hear older fishers talking of a GAFF which is an old-fashioned contraption used to stab the fish and haul it out of the water. Not very nice. It assumes you are not into catch and release. Then there's a TAILER, which is a loop of wire that tightens around the fish's tail, to lift it out of the water: interesting to know what it is, but stick to a net.

On to other bits of tackle you may come across. A WADING STICK is a must when in deep water or where the wading is bad. As for the smaller bits, a pair of

SCISSORS should be included. Make sure they have a rounded safety edge, especially if they're on a string around your neck. A BOX OF MATCHES is always useful, not least because the emery side can be used to sharpen fly hooks. A SAFETY PIN: useful for unpicking wind knots in the nylon. A SMALL PIECE OF CANDLE: good for rubbing on the rod joints, to stop them from slipping. Some STICKING TAPE: used to cover the joints for the same reason. A THERMOMETER: if you're a fussy fisher, you can test the water from time to time. A TORCH: it's easy to get carried away by the river and forget about time. MIDGE REPELLENT: vital for anywhere north of Newcastle. Some SWEETS and a HOT DRINK, perhaps some SANDWICHES, depending on how far from home you are. And it's sensible to keep a small FIRST-AID KIT in your car along with a dry TOWEL and a change of CLOTHES.

Finally, you'll need something to carry that fish home in and the proper name for this is a BASS. A bass is a salmon-shaped bag, usually made of straw or hessian, but you can improvise. Sometimes it tempts fate to take along a proper salmon carrier – just keep a large bin bag handy and you never know!

CHAPTER SIX

Clothing

'Fishing is a delusion entirely surrounded
by liars in old clothes.'

DON MARQUIS

Taking up fly-fishing is probably the best chance you'll ever have to join the Green-Wellie brigade and not feel self-conscious. For, if you have this idea of the archetypal game-fisher in his statutory plus-twos and tweed cap, you could well be right. There are folk who dress for the part, but, it has to be said, they're not necessarily the most successful fishers.

Take the story of the man who decided to take up fly-fishing as an antidote to the stresses and strains of a high-pressure city job. For two years, he threw himself whole-heartedly into the affair, buying all the right country clothes and tackle and going fishing as often as he could. The fact that he caught nothing – nay, didn't even have a single, solitary bite, didn't seem to deter him, until on one of his

fishing days he was out on a small river in the West Country, dressed to kill.

'It's not fair. The fish are lying at the other side of the river', he grumbled, 'and that's where I need to cast my line, but I can't get across in these thigh waders and this jacket's too long for the job!' As he spoke, there was a loud whistle and a young man sauntered by, casually dressed in a pair of cut-off jeans, a holed, woolly jumper and a pair of battered wellies. Over one shoulder was a rod and over the other was a stick, from which hung three large salmon. The city man was so demoralised, he sold his clothes and tackle and never fished again.

You, too, will see such scenes. Folk flogging away on a

" Clothes don't make a Fisher "

fancy river in their regulation jackets and waders and catching absolutely nothing. Then along comes a local, dressed as if he's out for an afternoon stroll and proceeds on the first cast to hook a whopper. It just goes to show that clothes don't make a fisher. Comfort is another thing and we'll go into that later, but as a beginner, don't spend money on anything until you know you like the sport.

So, if this is your first time by the river, see if you can cobble together something at home. If it's chilly, a couple of warm tee-shirts, a pair of jeans or cords, a thick woolly jumper and some warm socks will do fine. Beg or borrow a waterproof jacket and hat, add some wellies and you're ready to go.

As your interest grows, the time will come to invest in decent fishing clothes, and by decent, I mean warm and protective. True, there are glorious, dry days to be had by the river, but to be honest, when fishing for salmon, they're few and far between. The advice is to plan for wind, rain and snow, like the Victorians did. This century-old piece of sound advice was spotted in a fishing magazine.

When fishing in extreme conditions, leave the river every half hour and check your lower limbs. If they are scarlet, it is safe to re-enter the river; if blue, it is deemed unwise to continue, for to do so would result in loss of one, if not both legs and it is wise to wait until circulation has returned.

To avoid such an unlikely catastrophe, a beginner

should buy clothing that's practical, comfortable and recommended. Take advice from other fishers and the chances are, they'll probably start with a JACKET.

A decent jacket can last for years and judging by the worn, torn specimens paraded on river banks, many obviously do. People get attached to their old coats; there's a certain inverted country snobbery about wearing something that's not spanking new. Jackets come in all sorts of shapes and sizes, though the popular ones do seem to be the green, waxed-cotton types. Jackets also come in different lengths and the choice depends on the sort of fishing you plan to do. For example, long jackets protect legs from rain and wind and are fine for winter, or for fishing from the bank, or in shallow water, but they're not so good for wading in deep water. Shorter jackets are fine in summer, but then they don't give much protection in bad weather.

So, get something in-between, a middle length and go for a lighter rather than heavier weight. The fisher buying in the depths of winter might be tempted to get the heaviest, warmest garment he can find, but that isn't going to be much use if the weather improves and the work rate increases. Don't forget, you can always put extra layers underneath, such as a fleecy detachable lining, a padded body-warmer, or even an extra jumper; it's not so easy to make a heavy jacket lighter.

One last thought when choosing: do make sure your

jacket's got plenty of pockets, the more the merrier for a fisher, because we all need somewhere to put our fly-boxes, sweets and tissues.

The next item of clothing is a HAT or a HOOD. This is vital, not only for warmth, but also to protect the head from flies, both real and artificial. On really wet days, a hood stops water from trickling down your neck, but if you decide on a hat, there's no shortage of choice. A sou'wester, a peaked cap, a fancy cloche or even a Balaclava: there's nothing like a warm head, especially if you suffer in the cold. Perhaps the best of all, may be one of those peaked hats with earflaps which tie under the chin to keep the cheeks warm as well. They seem to be quite popular and can be found in rain-resistant fabric as well. It might leave you looking and feeling like a member of the SAS on a survival course, but in fishing, that's sometimes how it feels.

On to footwear, and here the angler needs something that's comfortable, robust and waterproof. Again, like the jacket, the choice will depend on where you plan to fish. If it's just from the bank, then WELLIES will do fine. But it's a feeble fisher who doesn't step out in the water at some stage, so you will almost certainly need to invest in a good pair of WADERS. Waders are basically extended wellies and there are two different sorts: those which come up to the thighs, THIGH WADERS, and those that come over the chest, CHEST WADERS. Thigh waders are held up with strips of rubber which clip to a belt or trousers. Chest waders have extendable straps which loop over the shoulder.

Thigh waders are easier to walk in than chest waders, but imagine the scene: you hook a small salmon and start to follow it downstream. It isn't a big one, but it's spring and the fish is a real live wire, pulling the rod this way and that, and yanking off great handfuls of line. You seem to be doing quite well in trying to control it, until it dawns that you're getting in deeper and deeper, with the water inching ever higher towards the tops of your thigh waders. Of course, in the panic to stay dry, you lose both your concentration and the fish – and get a good soaking into the bargain.

After that, you buy a pair of chest waders and are a convert. As well as keeping feet dry, chest waders are much warmer and can protect your back from the wind. (They also mean the angler can sit down on the river bank without getting a wet bottom!) But there are some disad-

vantages to chest waders: they can get extremely hot and sticky in summer and they're not the easiest things to walk about in, especially if it's a long trek from car to river. They can also be devilishly difficult to put on and take off, but it's a skill worth acquiring. Always bear in mind that should you fall into the river, they're probably not the best things to be wearing, as they can soon fill up with water.

That said, if you can only afford one sort, go for the chest waders, and pay a little bit extra for good ones – after all, you don't want things that leak at the seams after a few months. You also don't want anything that might pinch toes, so do go up at least half-a-shoe size. Feet encased in rubber are guaranteed to sweat and expand and in cold weather, there must be room for a couple of pairs of woolly socks. Remember what it's like standing in snow with wellingtons on? Well, double the chill factor in three feet of freezing water.

Which brings us on to NEOPRENES, which are ultra-warm, ultra-expensive waders. Basically they're a dry-suit which doesn't leave much to the imagination. In summer you will roast, but there's nothing warmer for the winter.

I know I keep harping back to this, but warmth is crucial when fishing, so another must are some GLOVES. Buy several pairs of thermal mitts, ones which are nice and warm but not so thick that you can't tie knots or feel the line. Always take along a spare pair, because it's surprising how soon gloves become waterlogged. It's no fun fishing

with cold, wet hands, but people find ingenious ways of keeping themselves warm and dry, including wearing rubber washing-up gloves over woollen ones.

A SCARF is another welcome addition to the angling wardrobe. If it's big enough, it can double as a hat. Just be careful to tuck everything well in, so there aren't bits of material flapping about to get in the way of the rod and reel.

As far as colour goes, I don't think there's any firm evidence that a bright red jumper will scare fish away, but a cream or white one might just glare on the water, so avoid

When all you're catching is a COLD....

those shades. Most fishing clothes are green or brown so as to blend in with the natural surroundings. Always take along more garments than you think you'll need; it's easy to take something off, but not so easy to warm up if there's only the one jumper. Also, always keep a set of dry clothes in the car. If you're really planning on going swimming, a towel may help too.

Finally, two items you must have with you. First is an angling LIFE JACKET. Quite smart, quite expensive, but it will keep you warm and it might just save your life in deep water. Second is a pair of GLASSES or SUNGLASSES. Polarised glass helps the angler see where fish are lying in the pool, but there's another reason to wear them: horrible accidents can happen and hooks can end up embedded anywhere. So, please, protect your eyes.

CHAPTER SEVEN

Putting it all Together

'Tis an affair of luck.'

HENRY VAN DYKE, *FISHERMAN'S LUCK*

Luck does play a great part in catching salmon. But if you're drawing a blank, there's often another reason. It could be you're not using the right tackle, or that the weather conditions aren't suitable, or, heaven forbid, you're just not good enough! Don't despair; a beginner may not have the necessary skills to guarantee a fish, but you can still give yourself a sporting chance by making sure your equipment is in good working order and properly assembled. The old maxim holds true: if you want a job doing, you must do it yourself.

Therefore, start as you mean to go on and learn to tackle up correctly, even though it might not always be

necessary. You may be especially lucky and have a ghillie on the beat, but some of the time, he may not be available. Also, if you can take responsibility for your own rod, reel and line, there'll be no-one else to blame if something goes wrong. Anglers have long memories: they never forget the fish that someone else lost them when they didn't tie the fly on tightly enough. In fact they will never be able to look at that person again without seeing a large salmon disappearing into the distance.

Another reason for becoming self-sufficient is that although it may be a struggle at first, it's much more satisfying to master the technicalities. Once you know the equipment and how it slots together, trips to the river will be more enjoyable and you'll be a confident fisher.

Of course, as a beginner, the temptation is to let the experienced fisher take charge and to spend the first year expecting whoever takes you fishing to sort out the problems. 'Oh, I don't know what's happened. My fly just seems to have disappeared. Do you think you could tie on another?' Or, 'Oh, what are these tiny knots in my nylon? Can you help me please?' Such requests are generally dealt with kindly. But don't expect anyone to look sympathetically upon you if you say, 'Look, I've got this favourite fly and when I cast back, it got tangled in that tree. Do you think you could shin up and get it down for me?'

And, as you go on, you'll realise that, although fishing is a companionable sort of sport, it can also be a solitary one.

Sometimes, a group of anglers will be casting fairly closely together, which means it's easy to ask for help. At other times, you might be a quarter of a mile from the nearest rod. It's then that you must start to iron out the problems.

You'll never regret becoming an independent fisher. It means if you wake up in the morning and decide to go to the river, you're not at the mercy of husband, wife, father, ghillie, the milkman, or whoever. You may still not be an expert fisher, but you'll be able to understand the tackle and do your own thing. Let's face it, you may be the best beginner in the world, but people do get tired of being asked to change flies, tie knots and generally nanny the novice, and who can blame them?

Fishers are generally accommodating people who will willingly help and advise others. But, at the end of the day, unless they're being paid specifically to look after you, or are quite doting, there will come a stage when they, too, will want to fish rather than fuss. At the very least, they'll want to see some sort of effort. That is, that you are also prepared to have a go at wading into the rough water to rescue a sunken fly, or crawling into the prickly gorse bush to untangle the line.

Incidentally, if you really get into desperate trouble and simply can't sort it out, always ask the more mature fisher for help. This riverside veteran has a wealth of local knowledge and patience. He's usually seen and done it all before and will be delighted to pass on a few old-timer's tips. As a beginner, the one to avoid is the younger, more aggressive angler. He is there for two reasons only: to demonstrate his prowess on the water and to catch fish – so he's unlikely to come to the rescue.

Let's put it all together then and tackle-up. We'll start with the rod. Because fly-rods are long and unwieldy, they're generally assembled at the water, but as a beginner, this won't do any harm. Have a wee practice run before you set off for the river and it might save a lot of embarrassment in front of other fishers. Do it in the open, where you won't hit anything.

So, take the rod from its sleeve. It'll usually be in three parts and you must slot the ends of these parts, the JOINTS, or FERRULES as they're called, firmly together, thin ends pushing into thicker ends. You should now have something resembling a complete rod which tapers. Take a good look: there's a thick handle at one end, which is called the BUTT and this is often covered in cork, or some non-slip material. In the middle of the butt, there's the REEL-SEAT – and this is where the reel sits. At intervals along the underside of the rod are small, round RINGS, through which the line is threaded. These get smaller as the rod narrows, with the final ring at the rod point sometimes called the TIP-RING. The only other thing of note on the rod is a tiny wire eyelet, just above the butt, which can be used as an anchor for the fly when the rod's being carried.

Now, check that the rings are aligned. When you look

down the length of the rod, they should be in a straight line. Waggle the rod about, taking care not to hit anything. It should feel firm but flexible. The ferrules on a new rod should be nice and stiff, but they'll soon loosen with use, sometimes with catastrophic results. Imagine the scene. You've staggered a mile in waders to a Scottish loch. There's been much huffing and puffing, but the thought of all those fish is enough to spur you on. Two hours later, you reach the top and start to lengthen the line before putting on a fly. Unhappily, on the first cast, the rod breaks in two. You haven't tightened one of the joints properly and can only watch as the top half flies off and goes sailing into the distance. You are on Loch Dubh, which in Gaelic means the Black Loch – and it is living up to its name.

You feel you're jinxed. But this sort of disaster can easily be prevented by rubbing the rod-joints with a piece of candle wax before slotting them together. The theory is that the wax acts as a seal and helps to stop any loosening. Some anglers make extra sure by sticking tape over the joints. But with all these precautions, don't be surprised if it's nigh on impossible to take the rod to bits again. Imagine a party of fishers trying to dismantle a rod that's been sealed: half-a-dozen or so of them, all huffing and puffing and pulling in different directions, trying to prise the rod apart. All they need is for one of them to put on a pair of rubber gloves and twist the offending portions apart. It never fails.

So, your rod is assembled, and you can be proud of yourself. Now lean it somewhere safe, where it isn't going to fall or knock against anything and turn your attention to the reel. As we already know from the chapter on tackle, a reel needs backing, line and leader, in that order. Backing is wound on first, followed by line, but joining these two together is a fiddly business and this is one task that's really not recommended for a beginner. Instead, ask the assistant in the tackle shop to do it for you. It won't be a problem. People in tackle shops are well used to such requests. Indeed, they often have small machines behind the counter, which will do in ten minutes what would take us mere mortals the better part of a day. And, of course, if they do it, you can fish with confidence.

The next step is to attach the reel to the rod. In the middle of the rod-butt is the reel-seat and you must slot the lower bar of the reel into the bottom ring of the reel-seat. Press the reel against the rod, slide the top ring back down and screw it firmly into place. The reel should be sitting securely on the rod, but do make sure it's the right way round. A right-handed fisher would usually have the handle on the right side. Someone left-handed will presumably want it sitting the other way. Also note that line and backing should be wound on according to whether you're right or left-handed, so tell the tackle shop assistant before he starts the job what your preference is.

Now, draw some line off the reel. It needs to come out

straight and not be bent round one of the reel bars or guides, otherwise it won't cast properly. Next, thread the line through the rod-rings. But again, be careful not to miss one out, because it's something that's easily done, and it'll drive you mad when everything's set up and you find that the line's jerking on each cast because you've missed a ring. Having threaded it through, pull out a couple of metres or so from the tip ring and then lie the rod down or lean it in a safe place where it won't fall over.

The line is now ready for its NYLON, or LEADER, though it's also referred to as a CAST. Leaders can be bought ready-made, but it's much cheaper to get a spool of nylon and make your own. So, take the spool of nylon and cut off a length. A very rough guide is two arm spans, but a better one is something that's roughly three-quarters the length of the rod. Always overestimate rather than underes-

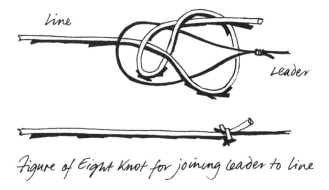

Figure of Eight Knot for joining leader to line

timate. To join leader to line, hold the nylon and tie a loop in the end. Then, take the line and push it through the loop with a FIGURE-OF-EIGHT KNOT (see diagram on page 59). If you have difficulty with this knot, find two lengths of rope and practice it on a big scale.

The final thing is to tie the fly to the end of the leader. There are many different knots in fishing, but one, which is basic and quite effective, is known as the HALF BLOOD or CLINCH KNOT. It goes as follows.

Put the nylon through the eye of the fly, bring it back and twist it round the main nylon half-a-dozen times and then push it back through itself (see diagram below). Some people, when they've twisted the nylon, spit on it. This is not a good luck ritual. It's what's known in the trade as GREASING the nylon, as it helps to reduce friction and heat, so there's less likelihood of a slip or snap when a fish

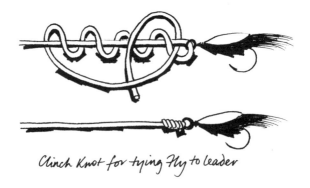

Clinch Knot for tying Fly to leader

is on and everything is straining.

You may be despairing, especially if you're not technical, but please, don't. The thing is, as a fisher, you only need to know a couple of simple knots, so long as they're tied securely. Having said that, there can't be an angler who hasn't at some stage doubted his own handiwork. In fact, no matter how many salmon are caught, when the moment of truth comes, there's always that niggling doubt. 'Was the fly tied on tightly enough? Will the knot hold?' Of course it will. It must!

So, the fly is on and it must be pulled tightly to make sure everything is secure. Don't use fingers or teeth, as that's a sure way to a nasty accident. Instead, take a pair of safety scissors, and holding them, place the closed blade in the bend of the hook and pull the leader with the other hand. Once the knot is tight, clip the fly hook to one of the rings on the rod, and start to reel in until line and leader are taut. Some people clip the fly to the small eyelet just above the butt, but anglers learn to their cost to avoid this little gadget, because they carry the rod by the butt – and if it's a big fly, with big hooks, the chances of catching themselves are high.

So, there you are. All tackled up and ready to go. But remember, you will often be fishing far from home. So before you go, it's worth making a check list. Beginners are enthusiastic and eager to get going – and that's good – but there's nothing worse than getting to the water and finding

a vital piece of tackle has been left at home. So make a list of the essentials and tick things off.

- Rod
- Spare line
- Nylon
- Scissors
- Waders
- Wading stick
- Rod licence
- Suitable clothes
- Reel with backing and line
- Spare reel
- Flies
- Net
- Lifejacket
- Fishing permit/licence
- Sunglasses
- Spare clothes/towel

Frankly, you won't need that much. Unlike coarse fishing or spinning, where the angler has to go armed to the teeth with all manner of weights and baits, fly-fishing is really quite economical on tackle.

Finally, it's as well to say here that there are many different schools of thought about how lines, casts and flies should be tied; all I've given is a simple selection, because to my mind, simplicity is the key to fishing. You too, may like to adopt the KISS philosophy. KISS – Keep It Simple, Stupid. Those who wish to know more about the finer points of knots and lines can consult a more expert book than this, or alternatively…a sailor.

CHAPTER EIGHT

Casting

'If your line's not in the water, you'll not catch fish.'

MY FATHER-IN-LAW, TOMMY POTTS

By now, you have some idea of how the tackle is put together. The next bit of the operation is to try it out. A first trip to the water can be daunting, but don't worry. Unless you fall out with other fishers, or into the river, it's going to be a wonderful day, so enjoy it!

With luck, you've arrived at a pleasant, peaceful spot, with an experienced angler at your side. Now, take the rod out of its sleeve, assemble it and put on the reel. Thread the line through the rod rings, tie on the nylon but instead of a fly, for safety, attach a small piece of cotton rag. For although casting looks very simple when watching someone else doing it, the reality is rather different. Some irritating people pick it up very quickly and never come to any harm. Others will serve many years of a long and frustrating apprenticeship and carry the scars to prove it! Casting is also difficult to describe in words and the only way to learn is by the water. Some people will advise practicing over fields or lawns. This is all very well, but it won't give the real feel of the art.

So here goes. Basically, the aim in fly-fishing is to project the fly at the end of your line and nylon over the water. Your rod is a means of projecting it across the river. This action is called CASTING. The plan is to fish over as much water as possible. Remember, too, anglers generally fish DOWNSTREAM. That is, in the same direction of the water flow. Like everything else in fishing, though, there are exceptions. Sometimes, you may be BACKING UP a pool and then, you will fish upstream. Of course, the beginner usually ends up fishing downstream, upstream and all over the stream. Infuriatingly, they might even catch a fish this way, but it is probably just luck. Unless told differently by an expert or a ghillie, you should always fish downstream.

So, starting at the head or top of a pool, you want to cast the line across the water. The current will bring the fly round in an arc and the object is to make it 'swim'. What we're trying to do is imitate one of the salmon's favourite foods. That's the theory, despite the fact we've already established that salmon don't feed in fresh water. Whatever, the fly must look lifelike and attractive. It can either imitate some plankton, a small fish, or a waterborne insect.

There are different ways of casting, some more complex than others. On some rivers you will see expert anglers (usually male) doing the Snake Roll and the Switch Cast. They seem to hurl around unimaginable lengths of line in elaborate circles. This is advanced casting. For you, the amateur who just wants to catch a salmon, you must start with the basics. And that means the standard OVERHEAD CAST. So, first of all, check there's nothing behind you – no trees or bushes to get in the way, or people and animals to maim. Make sure you're wearing glasses or sunglasses. Stand comfortably with feet apart. It's important to be well-balanced, as you don't want to end up falling over. Now, if you're right-handed, hold the rod firmly with the right hand in the middle of the cork grip.

Casting is an art....

Put your left hand on the butt a few inches below the reel. Get used to that. Waggle the rod around and up and down. Now, take your left hand off the butt and pull three or four metres of line off the reel. Put your hand back on the butt. Get the feel by lifting the line off the ground and throwing it forwards and back. When used to that, you can start to pause for a couple of seconds on the back cast, before trying to flick the rod crisply forward. This is not as easy as it seems and the line may end up wrapped around your head before very long. The pause on the back cast is very important. All rod actions vary, but try taking the line back and counting 'one-two' before bringing it forward again. Don't dither. Make movements firm and decisive, otherwise the line won't flow.

When you can throw the line a few metres in front of you the next step is to learn to SHOOT the line. To do this, pull off a few more handfuls of line and let them lie at the ground by your feet. Make sure your hands are where they should be on the butt. Now with the forefinger of your right hand, hold the line against the rod. Keep hold of the line as you cast back. Pause, then flick the rod forward with your wrist, release your forefinger and let the line go. It should go shooting through the rod-rings.

Shooting line is probably the most difficult action for any beginner to master, because the time the line is released is critical. Many people become very frustrated in trying to master the technique, but basically, casting is all down to

TIMING. It'll drive you mad trying to get it right, but it's a comfort to know that, rather like learning to hit a golf ball or ride a bike, everything gradually begins to fall into place. Don't get too confident, though. The experts may shoot out 30 metres and more and make it look as easy as pie. As a beginner don't be tempted to rush things. You'll get into an awful mess with spare line going here, there and everywhere and someone could get hurt. Wait until you can shoot a couple of metres before trying for more: in overhead casting, there are a host of things which can go wrong.

TAKING THE ROD TOO FAR BACK. This is a common problem. The rod should stop at the ear of the casting shoulder. Taking it any further may mean the line hits the ground behind, which will mar the cast, or worse still, break the fly on a stone or rock.

NOT USING BOTH HANDS TO WORK THE ROD. You need them, not for extra force, but to create the spring action required to cast out.

LOOKING BACKWARDS INSTEAD OF FORWARDS. When casting back, the line is meant to curl round in a loop before it comes forward again and it's tempting to reassure yourself by glancing over your shoulder. Don't do it! It'll put you off balance and spoil the forward cast.

POOR TIMING. As we've heard, the length of pause on the back-cast is vital. If the line cracks like a whip when

it comes forward, it may not have had enough time to straighten out behind. The sound you want to hear is a low, gliding whistle as the line runs effortlessly through the rings of the rod.

WIND KNOTS. These really are the scourge of the beginner. As the line flails about (as it surely will!) the nylon has a nasty habit of twisting itself into tiny knots. These must be taken out immediately, as they weaken the nylon: one thing if you don't mind losing a fly, but quite another when it comes to losing a fish. Wind knots are a nightmare to undo, by the way. It's often simpler to replace the offending length of nylon with a new bit, but if you don't like waste, here's a tip from an old ghillie. Use the tip of a safety pin or the point of a fly-hook to work the knot loose.

TRYING TOO HARD. Casting is a deliberate and rhythmical action, but if too much effort is used, it can defeat the purpose and prevent the rod from being given enough time to do its job. Watch a novice and they'll often be red-faced and bent double. Remember it's not yourself you're trying to throw into the water, it's the line and fly. Push with your wrists, never your shoulder. Keep a straight back. Never bow to the water. Let the rod do the work. You are there simply to guide it. Patience is the word. Patience and timing.

Now, if you're right-handed, you'll most probably have been casting over your right shoulder. But sooner or later, you'll find yourself trying to avoid bushes or

overhanging trees, or the wind and then it'll become clear why it's worth learning to cast off the other shoulder. This action feels most peculiar at first, rather like trying to write with the wrong hand. But it's worth persevering with, as it can mean the difference between being able to fish or not. Two of the biggest headaches in angling are trees on the bank behind you and the wind. Put them together and it spells trouble.

Just imagine the scene. A wonderful pool, and you've seen fish jumping. The water conditions are right for taking. Fellow fishers are optimistic and you're just in the mood to catch a big one. The problem is, there's a fierce wind blowing and each time you try to cast back, the line's being blown forwards again. Then the wind direction changes and the line starts flying round your neck and ears. You try to shift position, but it's hopeless, as the fly is blown in and out of gorse bushes and tree branches. So what do you do? Well, the fair-weather angler or faint-hearted beginner gives up, resolving to return when the weather improves. The more determined hang in there and look for an alternative cast.

The ROLL or SPEY cast has always been considered a rather difficult movement; a sort of stage two, which can only be perfected by ancient Scottish ghillies. However, the Spey cast is no longer a luxury. It's a necessity. As the late great fisher and writer, Hugh Falkus, wrote: 'It is a waste to equip yourself with expensive tackle and rent a costly beat, if you haven't the technique to take advantage of it. An ability to switch cast – that is to make roll, single-Spey and double-Spey casts – is essential to every salmon fisherman.' Put very simply, Spey-casting involves bringing the line towards you, but always keeping it in front, and then punching it energetically forwards. The theory is that the fly never gets hooked up in anything, as it never goes behind you and you can always see what it's doing. To my mind, it's a more difficult cast than the standard overhead cast, but once you have mastered this, you can move on to casts like the SNAKE ROLL and the SWITCH, and good luck to you.

But whichever cast is learnt, there's no substitute for practice and if you have problems, don't worry. You don't have to be a superb caster to catch a fish. What matters is enthusiasm and dedication. That said, it is immensely satisfying to be able to throw a good line, so do keep plugging away.

Now that you have some idea of casting, the next step is to learn what to do with the fly. That is, how to CONTROL it as it crosses the water. If you've been practising without a fly, now might be a good time to take off the cotton rag and put one on. But keep those sunglasses on.

How the fly is worked in the water is really a matter for the individual. Some anglers cast out and let the water current move it round. But it can be a good idea to inject some movement into the lure to make it lifelike. So,

standing at a slight angle to the river, cast out. The fly should land several feet in front and, as it swings round, with your left hand, pull in a few inches of line. Pause, then pull in a few more inches. Vary the speed, sometimes fast, sometimes slow. It will all give movement and life to the fly. This is called HANDLINING. It also helps to keep the line taut and this is important, because if a fish nudges the fly, you want to know right away and if there's masses of loose line everywhere, you may not feel it until it's too late. By the way, if the line looks bowed or crooked on the water, you must straighten, or MEND it. This is done by flicking the rod-tip to the side. Once the fly has reached the bank nearest you, the cast is complete. Always fish the line right round and leave it there for a few seconds before continuing. Who knows, a fish may have followed the lure and be just about to take, or there may be a fish lurking under the bank just waiting to bite. So, wait a minute and if nothing happens, get ready to cast out again. But before you continue, pause again. You will notice there is rather a lot of line lying on the water, far too much to cast back. So, pull in several feet and raise the rod slightly so that the water drips off. It makes sense that a shorter, lighter line is much easier to lift. The extra pause will also give time to compose yourself and think about the next cast – or even give that elusive salmon a final chance to take.

There's one further thought. When learning to cast, you will probably stand in one spot. But fly-fishers are

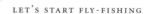

always on the move. A couple of casts and they walk a few yards downstream. Two more casts and they move on again. This is called COVERING the water and it gives a better chance of putting a fly over a fish. The theory is that you look for him, rather than the other way round. If the beat's a mile long, you'll be in for a lot of exercise, but that's just an added bonus!

Moving too slowly is a common fault for a beginner. It may mean only a quarter of the water is covered and only a quarter of the fish are caught. Never fish too long in one spot. It's very tempting, especially when you see a salmon jump, but it can be self-defeating, as you may just end up irritating whatever is there. Usually what happens is that you see a fish rise out of the water and then start to cast like mad over it. This is what's known as FLOGGING the water. In reality, what happens is that by your third cast, the fish has swum off to another corner of the pool, and by the time you're on your thirtieth, he'll be sniggering quietly whilst lazing under a stone by the far bank. The other reason, of course, to move on, is that there may be another angler coming up behind and he's unlikely to be amused if you stand still. Never obstruct another fisher or get too close to him. For a start, it's dangerous. Secondly, it's very irritating when someone hogs a good spot on the river.

There are a few final thoughts on casting. It's worth checking the fly every dozen casts or so, to make sure the hooks aren't broken or bent, or clogged up with weed. Or

that you've still got a fly there at all. You may, at some stage, find yourself casting without a fly; I hope you spot it earlier rather than later in the day! It's also worth checking your nylon for knots, kinks or fraying.

And finally, if the fly gets stuck, as it most certainly will, remember that brain is generally better than brawn. It may be stuck on a rock in the water, hanging from a tree, or wrapped round a prickly gorse bush. Brute force is not usually the answer. First try the gentle approach. Waggle the rod tip up and down to see if that loosens things. If not, put the rod down – never be tempted to use the rod to yank the line free. You might end up breaking it. Place it down somewhere safe, then wrap the line at the end around your arm and shoulder and pull. You may end up losing fly and nylon, but you should, at least recover the line.

There are other ways of getting out of the mess. One ghillie is known for the karate chops he gives to the rod butt before the fly comes free. Please don't try this. You'll probably break both rod and hand. It's infuriating when you're stuck: many trees will be scaled and river stones overturned before you're finished. But losing flies is part of fly-fishing, so the best thing to do is take along plenty of spares, for until you become a competent caster, you will certainly need them.

CHAPTER NINE

Catching, Playing and Landing a Fish

Angling: incessant expectation,
and perpetual disappointment.

ARTHUR YOUNG, *TRAVELS IN FRANCE*

You may be the best caster in the world by now, but if you want to catch something, you've got to use some cunning too. Just because there's some water about, doesn't mean there's necessarily anything in it.

Time and the elements conspire to thwart the salmon-fisher. As we already know, some rivers are only worth fishing at certain times and you will always turn up at the wrong place, on the wrong day. In other cases, weather conditions will be impossible and there won't be the slightest chance of tickling a tadpole, let alone seeing a salmon. So, before setting off, it's worth putting some effort into trying to find out what the chances are.

Some anglers are quite secretive about this, hoping to keep the best beats for themselves, but most are a fairly generous lot. Particularly useful are the people in local tackle shops, who'll reveal what's been caught locally, on which beats and at what time of day. Angling magazines, too, are useful guides. Read the river reports and articles for details of catches. Some people check on the time of tides, especially if they have a beat near an estuary and the fish are coming up on the fresh water. If travelling away to fish, ring up the local fishing hotel before you go. Sometimes they'll be quite honest and say, 'There's no water in the river, but rain is expected, so come!' Others will just want the custom and say, 'Yes, it's fine' and then, when you arrive, it'll often be a case of, 'You should have been here yesterday!' Yes, no matter how dedicated, it's awful to fish for days and see nothing. That said, there's no guarantee of success even if you can see the fish. Anglers have reported fishing in rivers while surrounded by jumping salmon – and still, they don't catch anything!

But we are assuming that there is at least one fish in the water, so go slowly and carefully. Salmon aren't as easily disturbed as some fish, like trout, but you've still got to tread carefully if you want to succeed. As it states in the book, *Fly-Fishing for Duffers*: 'Your chance of a fish is much greater if he doesn't hear, (if fish do hear), see or feel you, your footfall, your rod, line, cast, flash, reflection or shadow.' Always approach a pool with great care. It may be empty, true, but you don't want to risk scattering anything that might be in there by stamping or splashing about in waders. In the same vein, don't let dogs, children, grandma or whoever, laugh, shout, bark, or generally make a noise on the bank, as vibrations are easily transmitted. Some folk won't even slam a car door near the river. In the same vein, when boat-fishing, try not to splash the oars. Watch the old-timers, the ghillies and fishers of many years; they row as though they have all the time in the world, and it's not just because they've nothing else to do. Remember, you are the hunter, but the salmon has the upper hand, for he knows the nooks and crannies of his watery domain far better than any angler ever will.

Finding a fish can be a problem, for a beat can be a mile long – and that's an awful lot of water to cover when you're just taking pot luck. Basically, salmon can be found in almost any part of the water, but there are areas where there might just be a better chance of catching one. For example, you'll often hear experienced anglers talking of a good POOL or a good LIE – that's a place where the fish does just that. Perhaps he wants a break from his run upstream and has found a large rock to shelter behind before moving on, or maybe there's a deep, cool pool to laze about in. Whatever the reason, a lie can certainly be one of the best spots to fish over, which is all very well, if you happen to know where this fruitful place is. Another good area might be a STREAMY bit, for salmon are sometimes found in the rough water. All very confusing. But the comforting thing to remember is, if they're coming upstream, sooner or later they'll swim past your fly, so keep it wet and keep it moving.

The next thing to know is that salmon ARE found on BOTH sides of the water. As a novice, it may seem the grass is always greener on the other side, because you're always being told to cast your fly to the fish lying on the far bank. Well, that is often the case, but sometimes, just occasionally, the fish actually lie on your side. Then, you don't have to try as hard. And this brings in the question of how far a fisher should wade across a river, especially if he only has fishing rights for one side of the bank. To my mind, he should go no further than half-way. There's nothing more infuriating than arriving to find that someone from the opposite bank has taken the liberty of wading over to your side, so you find yourself fishing rod-tip to rod-tip.

However, let's set the scene. It's a good fishing day, slightly overcast, with a gentle breeze ruffling the water. You have tried to read the river and have some idea where the salmon may be resting. You've found a good spot and have waded in. You cast back and the line shoots straight out front. The red and black, half-inch double goes swimming tantalisingly downstream, when suddenly, there's a sharp pull. A fish! Or is it?!

People say, 'When you catch a salmon, there'll be no doubt, you'll just know'. Well, I'm afraid you might not 'just know'. Instead, the scene may go like this. The fly is hooked to something and you are convinced it's a fish. The thing is, it seems so realistic. Each time you wind in, the line pulls out again, all the time moving and jerking about. You know there's a fish on the end, but you can't make any sense of it. In the end you accost some nearby walkers. 'Please, I've got this enormous fish on. Get help quickly!' And off they run to fetch another angler, who puts down his rod and hurries along, net at the ready. And when he gets there, he takes one look at you, red-faced and straining and he starts to laugh. 'Log', he says. A what?! A log, you have hooked not a fish, but a log.

We've all done it, including one local doctor who was out fishing in the village. The reel was screaming and the rod bent double and the word went round that he had on a whopping great salmon. The locals hadn't seen such excitement for years and, one by one, they downed tools and made for the river to witness the exciting event. What a marathon! It took our hero two hours to bring his catch to the net and when he did, a great cheer went up from the assembled crowd, especially when they realised that what he'd been playing wasn't the salmon of the century, but an old bucket, weighted with cement. That's a true story and many other fishers will tell tales of hooking hot-water bottles and plastic bags – and in one case, a set of false teeth!

So it's not that easy. Maybe for the experts, yes, but you and I can be forgiven when it comes to catching a salmon. After all, it depends on how a fish takes the fly, and as to what the rod feels like. For example, some of the more energetic types go straight in and whack! The line's reeling violently and you're left struggling to control the rod. Others are more gentle, simply toying with the fly, tugging

' JAWS - the big One! '

and sucking at it as they try to work out whether it's worth swallowing. Whatever happens, if there's movement at the end of the rod, there may be something there and if it really is a fish, it'll be the most exciting thing of all. The rod-tip may start to judder and the line begin to stream off the reel and the temptation for the beginner must be to do something, at the very least to shout wildly for help, or to raise the rod, but this opens up a whole new debate. To STRIKE at once, or to wait?

This is a controversial field. Some people say wait and give a salmon line, because by raising the rod and striking at once, you may pull the fly straight out of the fish's mouth. They will tell you to let the salmon suck in the fly, then, as he turns and takes the line with him, the hook will be set and he'll be well and truly caught. However, there's nothing like angling for divided opinions and the opposite view is that the fisher should strike as soon as he feels a pull. Strike before the fish has a chance to spit out the hook.

But wait or not, let's assume you have struck and the fish is well and truly hooked. The next step is to PLAY him, a rather unfortunate term, as this is not a game. What it means is that the fish will be trying to get off the hook, while you are trying to get him to the shore. And here you'll find that, just as salmon TAKE in different ways, they also react differently to being caught. Some stronger, fresher fish go careering up and down a pool, diving in and out of the water. Others come quietly and allow themselves simply to be led to the bank. Again, there are different ways to play a fish, but here are a few simple tips.

KEEP IN CONTACT WITH THE FISH. This is done by holding the rod-tip up, which keeps the line taut and the hook well-embedded. If the line were slack, you'd have no real feel as to where the fish was going.

LET THE FISH RUN. If a fish wants to move, let him. Simply spool out some line and let him run. The object is to tire him out, unless he tires you out first, which is always a possibility. There are fishers who have played a salmon for several hours before aching arms and throbbing backs force them to concede defeat. Then they must simply cut the nylon and their losses. But what a horrible thought: not just the idea of losing the fish, but the fact that he must swim off with a hook in his mouth.

DON'T LET HIM GET UPSTREAM. Your chances of him getting away are much greater if this happens. Try to keep him at a manageable downstream distance.

'Keep your rod-tip up! Wind in, wind out!' When you hook your first salmon, there'll be no shortage of advice. The instructions will be endless, but at some stage, whether it's a few minutes or a few hours, you'll wind in and, suddenly, feel less resistance. It appears the salmon has tired and may even be coming slowly towards the bank. Now you are about to LAND him, but don't be surprised if, on approaching the bank, he senses danger and takes off again. These fish have great stamina and the fight is by no means over yet. You may watch a fellow angler reel in a fish that looks for all the world like it is spent. But each time it comes in sight of the gravel bank, it gives an impassioned lurch, kicks its tail and is off again. Indeed, with a salmon on the end of the line, there'll be all sorts of worries. For example, will the nylon hold? Is the fly tied on properly, or will it work loose? Will the rod, which is straining like mad, break in half? Will the fish pull so hard he'll simply straighten the hook and get off? The list of things that can go wrong is endless. However, on this occasion, let's be optimistic and assume that everything holds and that the rod, despite being bent double, doesn't snap. In fact, you really seem to be getting the upper hand and the fish is tiring.

Now, for the next crucial bit and again, let's assume that as a beginner you have help. The fish is played out and brought to the bank. Now it's the turn of the NET. If it's lying elsewhere, ask your helper to retrieve it. Despite the tension, remember to be polite. 'Get the damn net, for God's sake!' is not a good thing to say to someone about to be entrusted with the job of landing your first salmon. When they return, ask them to slide the net under the surface of the water. Never be tempted to follow the salmon with the net; it will just frighten it instead. Keeping the rod tip up, bring the fish to the surface and lead it gently across the current and over the net. Then all the helper needs to do is lift both net and fish out of the water and onto the bank. It sounds a simple operation, but it can easily go wrong. Landing a fish is fraught with danger and it needs a clear head and some calm. Do not ask nervous people to do it, or folk with drink in them. And try not to ask people who are short-sighted and without their glasses.

If there is the slightest doubt that the person who's helping might make a mess of things, then do the job yourself. Hold the rod in your right hand, (unless you're left-handed, of course) and the net firmly in the other. Some folk put a small stone in the bottom of the net, so if it's windy, it keeps it steady and stops it turning inside out. Now bend slightly, all the time trying to keep the rod tip up, and place the net in the water. Slowly bring the fish over the net and lift it firmly out and onto the bank – well up onto the bank.

When you catch your first salmon, there will always be a degree of panic, but with luck, a helper will be there to

'WRONG AGAIN!'

advise. When you catch your second, Murphy's Law will decree that the helper has gone home and the net is in the car a quarter of a mile away. So you must now learn to land a fish without either. Quite simply, in this predicament, look for somewhere to beach it. It may be a spit of gravel or a grassy ledge by the water's edge. Again, make sure the fish is played out. Wind in some line, then walk the fish to the landing spot and gently pull it out of the water onto the grass or gravel. It will flap about, but loosen off a bit of line and walk behind him and you should be able to pick it up by the tail and lift it clean away from the water.

So there you are. You have hooked, played and landed a salmon and now it's there, a decision must be made. Game fishers have traditionally killed and eaten their catches, but these days more and more are being put back. It's called CATCH AND RELEASE and is becoming increasingly popular with fly-fishers, particularly on rivers where the salmon population is dwindling. You may have mixed views on this. Do you want to play a fish at the end of the line simply for the fun of it? Is this what game fishing is about? Surely a good salmon that's caught fairly should be eaten. On the other hand, if everyone took every fish they ever caught, how could the salmon ever hope to survive?

I think it goes like this. You have already caught one or two fish. Don't be greedy. You may not eat fish or know anyone who does. In that case, why take it? It's a small fish – so put it back. Let it live and grow and perhaps you will hook it again in two years when it's bigger. A kelt, we would not take, we already know that. And don't be tempted to take black or red fish. They probably won't taste good anyhow. Most important, if it's autumn, always spare a female fish that's about to spawn. She will be fat and full of eggs and possibly reddened. You will recognise the female because, unlike the male fish, she does not have a KYPE, which is a long pointed bit hanging from the lower jaw. You must also return a fish that is FOUL-HOOKED, that is, it is hooked somewhere other than in the mouth. All the above should go back and this is an operation in itself.

Here are some rules for catch and release, drawn up by angler and writer, Len Colclough.

- DON'T OVERPLAY A FISH. Use just enough pressure to bring it to the net without exhausting it.
- AVOID HANDLING A FISH OR TAKING IT FROM THE WATER. If you have to net your catch, use a KNOTLESS NET and keep it submerged.
- USE SMALL, BARBLESS HOOKS.
- HELP A TIRED FISH TO RECOVER. Never touch it with dry hands. Cradle the submerged fish until it can manage to swim off again.
- RELEASE IT IN RUNNING WATER where possible, to help it to revive.
- DO NOT RETURN A FISH WITH BLOOD FLOWING FROM THE MOUTH OR GILLS. It's going to die anyway and it's kinder to kill it.

If the hook is well down the fish's mouth, do not attempt to remove it. Simply snip off the leader and return the fish to the water. The hook may work its way out later. Remember, THE BEST HANDLED FISH IS THE LEAST HANDLED ONE.

But, if it's a silvery, healthy fish and your first, you may want to keep it. The thing is, not to stand dithering, but to make a decision. For a fish must be dispatched as quickly and humanely as possible. The proper instrument used for this is a PRIEST. A priest resembles a small, heavy truncheon, but a stone or a piece of wood will do the job as well. So, take whatever you're using, roll the fish onto his stomach and give a couple of short sharp taps just above the eyes. That should suffice. Now cover it up, away from sun and flies. Your first salmon! At this stage, you will either be filled with great remorse and vow never to kill another living thing again. Or there'll be a sense of elation and achievement and a longing to get back into the water to catch another.

But, even if you don't catch a fish, you may come close to it. And terms that might inspire are a PULL or a TOUCH. These are heartening words for a salmon-fisher, as they mean that a fish has at least toyed with the fly, maybe sucked it in and then let it go. Whatever way, it means there's been some interest, so the fly must have looked lifelike and appetising. In the same way, if you cast out and see something jump, you may have RAISED or MOVED a fish and this is also heartening for the angler.

And finally, are there really such things as perfect fishing conditions? Simple answer, no. But here's a few that might help.

- FISH AFTER A SPATE WHEN THE RIVER'S DROPPING, because the salmon are being roused into activity and are being drawn upstream.

- SALMON DON'T LIKE THE SUN'S GLARE, so they tend to sit in shady places.

- SALMON ARE MORE LIKELY TO TAKE A FLY WHEN THEY'RE RESTING IN A POOL.

- SALMON MOVE IN THE DARK, so night or dawn can be excellent taking times.

- RAIN IS GOOD and a most magical taking time is when a river first begins to rise, after the snow melts or there's a heavy downpour.

- THE AIR MUST BE WARMER THAN THE WATER. Everyone agrees on this. Some anglers are quite scientific, taking a thermometer for precise figures. To my mind being too technical takes away from the mystery of the sport. You will find your own way.

CHAPTER TEN

Looking after your Tackle

'I wonder if the fish goes home and boasts about the size of the bait he stole.'

ANON

If you've got this far, it will be dawning that salmon-fishing isn't a cheap pastime, so it's really worth looking after your tackle. The great thing about angling is that it's a companionable sport and we're often found in groups huddled in fishing huts, with our bags and clothes all heaped together. As a beginner, with lots of lovely new tackle, it's worth marking things, so you know what's what. Jackets are fairly easy to identify. 'Mine's the one with the rip across the pocket…' and so on. It's the wellies and waders that can be a problem, so write your name in waterproof ink on the inside of each boot. But, names do not impress thieves, so please, don't leave expensive tackle in unlocked cars, or obviously on show. Cover it up with a rug and always lock the doors. Even if fishing just a hundred yards down the bank, you never know who'll be passing by. It's a wretched thing to have to be on your guard in the countryside, but there it is.

Folk get very attached to their angling bits and bobs and some are particularly prized. Take Commander William Donald of Keswick, a former naval officer and an ardent fisher, who was devoted to his blue-green, high-necked jumper. It was the start of World War II and every good woman in the land who wasn't digging was knitting, carefully making jumpers and scarves for the men on the front line. Willie was in Scotland, preparing to set sail on his ship, when a crate of woollens arrived. Knitwear was gratefully received by all the servicemen, but especially by the seamen, for a winter on the ocean could get to even the hardest soul. Well, it was duly distributed, but when Willie got his, there, pinned to the inside of the blue-green jumper, was a small note, which read: 'With best wishes from Her Majesty the Queen, Buckingham Palace, 1939'. He wore it proudly and it kept him warm and safe throughout the war. And when the fighting finished and he could turn to happier things, the royal jumper went where the now Queen Mother, a keen angler herself, would probably most liked to have seen it go. It became Willie's

fishing jumper, and once again, it proved lucky. He was wearing it when he caught his first salmon, appropriately fishing on Royal Deeside, and he wore it when catching many more. Sadly, the said garment is no more. Had it been around, it would surely have been snapped up by a museum, for I don't know how many jumpers the Queen Mother has knitted in her time, but it can't be a great number. No, when it became too holed and snagged, a decision had to be made. What was to be done with the Queen Mother's jumper? Well, they couldn't possibly throw it in the dustbin. So after much thought, Willie respectfully cremated the remains in the garden.

Willie guarded that jumper for many long fishing years and was careful not to leave it anywhere or lend it to anyone. You may end up feeling the same about a lucky hat, or a pair of favourite gloves. You see, the problem is, that after a bit of wear and tear, most angling clothes tend to end up looking the same. Having said that, fishing gear is generally hardy, but you can still do your bit to prolong its life.

For example, WADERS and WELLIES must be properly dried out after each fishing trip and that means hanging them up. Left on the floor in a crumpled heap, they'll start to rot, or dry out all creased, which means the fabric's more likely to crack and leak. When putting waders away, hang them on a hook. Upside down is best, with boot clips attached to the sole, or good old-fashioned string.

(The airing cupboard is an excellent place for wet waders, but don't leave them there for too long.) Keeping them off floor level also deters unwelcome visitors. Leave waders in a garage cupboard for the winter and you may come back to find a family of field mice nesting down in the feet. Rather sweet, you might think, if only they hadn't chewed the expensive, felt-lined soles to make a cosy bed. In the same vein, if you don't like spiders, shake out your boots before you put them on.

Come to think of it, there's another good reason to hang up waders, and that's a social one. Fishing can be hot, sweaty work, and I defy anyone encased in rubber to plod for miles, then fish for hours and still come up smelling of

roses. Of course, you may get so carried away with the day that you don't realise. There you are in the fishing hut, with a strange smell in the air. Is it damp earth? The water not as fresh as it should be? The dog? Anything and everything will get blamed and it's only when the smell follows you into the bar at the end of the day, that it dawns what's happened. Socks can be washed. But let boots get damp time after time and they never recover and the only answer will then be a new pair – or some new friends!

A final note on waders. Don't expect them to last forever, because however careful folk are, they are prone to wear and tear. Their life can be extended with a wader MENDING KIT, which is a little box of plastic or rubber patches which glue over a hole or a tear. Alternatively, try some LIQUID MENDER which comes in a tube and hardens over the hole.

And so to JACKETS, which are rather more resilient than waders. But they, too, deserve a bit of kindness. Fishers will get wet and it's surprising how long a sodden jacket takes to dry out completely. If it's waxed, it'll need to be re-waxed at some stage if it's to stay waterproof. Dry cleaners will do this for you, but you can also do it yourself, although it's not a job for the faint-hearted.

As for other fishing clothes, look after your bits and pieces and they'll last much longer. If GLOVES, SOCKS, HATS, etc. get wet, dry them out. When the next time comes to fish, you'll be glad you did. In the same vein, don't leave soaked accessories in pockets or bags. Watch for rips, as woolly socks and jumpers are easily pulled when fishing. Just climb a few barbed-wire fences or get too near a large fishing hook, and you'll find out how easy it is. If things do rip, sew them – sooner rather than later. Left alone and a tiny hole can became a great big one, which may mean your favourite fishing jumper is consigned to the cat basket. Then even the cat will turn its nose up, as the smell promises something it never delivers.

As for tackle. You may like to MARK your ROD with an indelible pen, but alas, if it's stolen, the chances of getting it back are slim. The smaller things are the ones to watch out for. Put REELS, FLIES and FLYBOXES together and they can all look much of a muchness. A reel is fairly easy to mark, but you obviously can't do this with thirty flies and fifty metres of nylon. And to be quite honest, it would look a bit Scrooge-like to arrive at the river having tagged every hook, line and sinker. As far as these smaller items are concerned, just be careful when it comes to gathering together everything at the end of the day. Bags, baskets and fly-boxes all look fairly similar, and you don't want to lose stuff. In the same way, do try to return lent tackle, no matter how small or inexpensive it might seem. People do remember and might not be quite so eager to help next time. If you lose a borrowed lure, replace it, either with something similar, or the offer of a compensatory drink.

Borrowing flies and hooks and old tackle is one thing,

but it is unwise to ask to use someone's brand new carbon fibre rod. As we know, they're ultra-light and easy to carry, but they're also expensive and easily broken and the slightest knock can leave them, and you, shattered. So, here are some tips.

- When travelling to the river, make sure the rod's safe, somewhere where it can't be sat on, or squeezed. It's very tempting in all the excitement to throw it into the back of the car. But it's worth remembering that even if the rod's not actually broken, just a small bump can cause it to crack and weaken and the next time a line is cast, you may end up disappointed.

- Again, when the rod's up, watch where it's standing. Do not lay it on the ground where someone might accidentally stand on it. Do not put it in a place where it might slide over and break. You may be by the water, discussing the day with other fishers, when someone lets out a cry of horror and all heads spin to see a beautiful and expensive 15-footer slowly sliding off the bonnet of a nearby car. Despite a desperate rush to save it by its owner, a £300 classic ends up on the ground, completely shattered.

- Do watch where the rod is put. And remember that when it's taken down, its proper place is in its SLEEVE. Solid metal or leather tubes will protect a rod from almost anything, but a basic cloth cover is certainly better than nothing and should prevent

scratching and chipping. Again, if you're in a hurry, it's tempting to throw the rod in the back of the car and think, 'Oh, I'll put it away later.' Don't. Put it away at once, with the butt end downwards and the fragile tip pointing upwards. It must sound very virtuous and to be honest, every fisher has dropped or knocked over a rod at some stage, with varying results. Touch wood, your's won't suffer any permanent damage for the odd mishap, but you never know – the next fishing trip could be the one that leaves you cursing. And that is fatal. A 17th-century proverb goes:
If you swear, you will catch no fish.

One final thought: when carrying the rod, hold it by the butt, with the rod-tip slanted backwards. It means you're less likely to poke someone's eye and less likely to break the delicate tip-end by bumping into something. Likewise, when following a fisher who is carrying a rod this way, always allow a little room in case he or she comes to an abrupt stop. Carrying it like this also reduces the risk of getting the line tangled up in overhanging branches.

And so to REELS, which are hardier than rods, but again, neglect them at your peril. You may arrive at the river, eager to fish, only to find the spool grinding away in a most disconcerting way. You open it up to investigate and find the inside all rusted up. Ruefully, you recall a previous fishing trip when you slipped off a rock and into the river and gave both rod and reel a soaking. And then when you

got home, you thought you'd leave it to dry on its own. It didn't and it's a painful lesson. The fishing conditions are excellent, the weather just right, the water teeming with fish, but as there's only the one reel, the day is wasted. The moral is, keep your tackle dry and use the odd drop of oil or grease to keep everything turning. And, remember, if reels are wary of water, they simply hate sand, so never put a reel down on any surface that is grainy or sandy, because after that you might as well be grinding a pepper mill!

Ideally, you should check tackle after every fishing trip, but the end of the season is the time to take stock of what's there, what's missing and what needs repairing. When those boots are hung up as winter comes on, it's good to make sure that everything's left spick and span for a return in the spring. So as soon as the season's over, make a checklist. Do it at once, or you'll forget, especially in the run up to Christmas. It might involve examining flies and ordering new ones, or checking hooks to see barbs are present and correct Don't keep stuff that's damaged, though it's very tempting to do so. If a fly that started off with three hooks now has only two, throw it out; with a broken hook, all a fish may have to do is shake its head and it's away. And if a fly has lost most of its feathers, turf that out too. If it is your lucky lure, then keep it for sentiment and get it framed. But a damaged fly is no longer the fly you once fished with.

As for the heavier tackle, check rods and rod rings for

signs of cracking. They can then be wiped down and placed back in their sleeves. Reels should be dismantled and lightly oiled. Line should be taken off the spool and checked for kinks and frays. As far as leader goes, most experts recommend that left-over nylon should be thrown out at the end of the season, as it can weaken and rot. Be safe rather than sorry and buy a new batch every year. It's cheap enough.

And if YOU really want to survive another season, it's a good idea to clear out debris from tackle boxes and bags, as you'll be surprised what accumulates in a few months. Corners of old egg sandwiches, sticky toffee papers, ragged bits of tissue, broken hooks, a dried up apple core or two, or even a flask of three-month-old coffee may be some of the things you find. I know, because I have. You may even discover the reason behind that awful smell in the fishing cupboard.

CHAPTER ELEVEN

Safety on the Water

One, two, three, four, five
Once I caught a fish alive.
Why did I let it go?
Because it bit my finger so.

ANON

Whilst it's most unlikely you'll actually get bitten by a fish, there are real dangers in fishing. It may not be motor racing or skydiving, but it can still be dangerous, or at the very least, painful.

We're dealing with water here, every cubic centimetre of which weighs one gram. Doesn't sound much does it? Well, let's think about it. A cubic metre of water will therefore weigh 1,000kg. Now, imagine a tea-chest measuring one metre all-round. That volume of water will weigh one metric tonne. Imagine that same tea-chest moving towards you at walking pace. How heavy are you? I'll bet you're not even a tenth of the weight of that tea-chest. Could you stop it in its tracks? No. Now think of a carpet of these chests perhaps twenty metres wide and...well, that's the point really, their length in a flowing river is never-ending. Water is heavy and when it moves inexorably, it is enormously powerful.

Water is one of the primary natural forces in nature; it shapes our landscape and can have dominion over our way of life. Salmon rivers are often deep and currents can be treacherous. Great care is needed and flowing water must be treated with the utmost respect. It could happen like this: you arrive at the water to find your normally chatty ghillie full of doom and gloom and issuing dire warnings. It turns out he's been looking after one of his regular parties of fishers. As always, he'd placed them at various points along the beat, but one of the party, a young man in his thirties, was never seen alive again. When the ghillie came back to check, he'd simply disappeared. His rod and hat were found floating in the water, but it was several days before his body was recovered near the mouth of the river.

No-one will ever know exactly what happened. This river, the Tay, is notoriously dangerous in parts, with deep pools and strong, swirling currents. One minute, you're fishing in just a few inches of water, but the next step can take you well out of your depth. Another tragic story concerns the man who was sitting fishing in a small boat on a loch. He hooked a fish and in his excitement to play it, he stood up, overbalanced and fell in. The police divers discovered his body.

Those are drastic and horrible examples, I know, but I'm sure that almost every fisher can tell of his own personal scare in the water. Even a stretch that's harmless can turn nasty. You might be wading along quite peacefully, casting without a care in the world, when suddenly, the river bed falls steeply away – and there you are, struggling to stay upright and not lose your footing. Trying to turn back to the shore, the current pushes you along and all the time your waders are filling up and panic is taking hold. So get a life – and get a LIFE-JACKET, even if you know the river. You may be the best swimmer in the world, but weighed down by sodden clothes and filled waders in a raging stream, could you really cope? Such is the concern about safety now that some rivers won't let anglers on the water unless they're wearing a life-jacket.

Of course, the trick is to avoid falling in at all. Wading on slimy and slippery stones is a precarious business, but there are aids to help the angler stay upright and so preserve, at the very least, dignity, and at best, life. For example, there are boots with felt ANTI-SLIP soles. Expensive for sure, but how much do you value your life? Or another life-saver is a WADING STICK. This is a long pole made of wood or plastic, which is used to feel the way along a river bottom or as a 'steady' when the current gets strong. It should be sturdy and weighted at the bottom, otherwise, it'll float away in the stream and you'll spend half your time trying to retrieve it. A good stick will also have a loop at the top, which slips over the shoulder, so it won't get in the way when you're casting.

Take a leaf out of an old sailor's book, a former sea captain who regularly fishes, but always with life jacket and wading stick. Somehow, when you start fishing for salmon, you're keen to buy the exciting things, like the rod and the reel. The life-jackets and wading sticks just don't seem that important, particularly if you're younger. Well, any experienced fisher will say they're not just necessary, they're a vital part of the kit. So don't make the mistake of thinking fishing aids are just for the old and doddery. Water is no respecter of age, any age. The advice is never to underestimate the power of the river, or get too familiar or daring. Anglers need a certain amount of caution and lots of commonsense and that means judging pools and, if they're too deep for comfort, not risking it. Don't forget also that water levels rise and what's safe at midday might not be so later in the day.

One final thought. If you do find yourself in trouble without a stick, but with a net, improvise by holding the round end and using the handle as a steady until you reach the shallows. If stickless and netless – and really in a jam – use the rod to steady you home. It won't do it any good and should be considered a last resort. But if the rod breaks and you get to the bank, you can always buy a new one. If you break it and don't make it, it won't matter anyway. However, we're assuming you do make it, so wipe down the rod, dry the reel and grease it before it starts to rust.

From the water to the tackle, because that, too, can do a fair bit of damage. Take a fly-hook. Once a barb goes in, it's nigh-on impossible to get out. You may be fishing on a lovely autumn day, with dozens of silvery salmon dancing around in the water. You know you're bound to catch something and having just mastered the art of tying knots, you feel pretty confident. So you decide to change fly and start to put on a lovely orange Ally's Shrimp. You pull the knot tight, when you tug a little too enthusiastically and the hook goes right into your finger. Being stabbed by a fishing barb certainly isn't the most pleasant experience, but the upshot of the day is that the fishing's abandoned in favour of a trip to the local cottage hospital. You think you'll be a great novelty in casualty, with a gaily coloured salmon fly poking out of your finger. But when you get there, there's a huge queue of anglers all with hooks embedded in various parts of their body. After a horrible afternoon, you go home older and wiser and just grateful it wasn't your eye. The worst thing is the anti-tetanus jab they give you as you can't sit down for a week afterwards.

So, please, use the end of a pair of scissors to tighten a knot on a fly. Never, ever use teeth to cut nylon. It just takes the rod to fall over or someone to jerk it and the nylon could slide through your mouth and the fly into your cheek. Indeed, flies have been known to pierce cheeks, ears and even eyes, especially when the wind's blowing. This is certainly one of the most dangerous times, when the angler's throwing around lengths of line and nylon with a sharpened barb at the end. Always, always, wear glasses or sunglasses! They'll help to protect eyes. As hats help to shield faces and ears. To avoid costly law suits, please be aware of what's happening around you. Otherwise, you may end up hooking not only another angler, but also some innocent passer-by. In the same way, if watching someone else fishing, then stand well back. If you must stand close, because you're being taught, then tuck in as closely as possible to the opposite side of the shoulder the instructor's using. And never sneak up behind another angler when he's casting. Always give some warning.

And as you take care when casting, watch out when carrying the rod. Remember, it's got a thin, pointed tip, which can easily poke out an eye. Carry it with the POINT FACING BACKWARDS and again if you're following someone who's carrying a long rod, then keep well back. Don't forget, 15 feet goes an awfully long way. Take especial care when putting up the rod, or waving it around in the air, especially where there are POWER LINES about. There've been many cases of anglers being electrocuted this way, as modern rods are great conductors of electricity. Watch out in remote country areas, where power lines are often low and can be found in courtyards outside houses or hotels.

This is the countryside, so beware ELECTRIC FENCES. Beware, too, ELECTRIC STORMS. Lightning striking the rod and burning the angler to a frazzle sounds melodramatic, but it's not as impossible as it sounds. In a storm, seek shelter as soon as possible and don't stand there clutching the rod.

On a less dramatic note, fishing involves following the country code and that means TAKING HOME LITTER and SHUTTING GATES. It also means watching out for animals, especially where cattle and sheep might be standing near the river bank. Take heed of the tale of the man who was fishing without much success, when in desperation, he decided to swap his expensive feathered fly for the Garden Fly (*aka* the garden worm – much

'WATCH WHERE YOUR PUTTING IT!'

disapproved of by the purists). So, the beastie was placed on the hook and our angler cast back. As he fished, he kept lengthening his line. But suddenly, the line went too far back and hit the ground, where it was seized on by a passing hen. The next thing he knew, he was fishing with The Flying Chicken, as the poor old bird came sailing overhead. Who got the bigger fright, I am not quite sure.

Finally on the subject of animals, one of the most important rules is NOT TO LEAVE BITS OF NYLON LYING ABOUT. When a leader is changed, take the old one home and throw it in the dustbin. If you find another angler's cast hanging from a tree, take it down and dispose of it safely. It's another chore, I know, but if nylon is just discarded, it can cause great suffering to birds and small animals that may get tangled up in it.

Onto one of the particular perils of fishing. The

dreaded MIDGE. You can just see the scene. A quiet summer's evening and you're at the river, totally at peace with the world, when suddenly, you're attacked by an army of flying insects. Scottish midges are the worst. How such a tiny insect can inflict such monstrous bites is beyond belief. So slap on the ANTI-MIDGE CREAM, especially in late spring and summer. Better still, if heading for the Highlands, take a hat with an overhanging veil. NETTLES are not pleasant. Nor are BEE or WASP stings, but these are part and parcel of country life. Just watch where you sit and walk and keep a small FIRST-AID kit in your car.

Two other points. If fishing at night on your own, then tell someone where you're going. Then if something awful happens like a broken ankle, at least someone can raise the alarm. Lastly, although fishing and alcohol can go very nicely together, whisky and water can be a lethal combination. So, even though it's tempting to celebrate a catch with something suitable, it is sensible to save the drams until the end of the day.

And finally, please, please don't be put off by this chapter of doom and possible gloom. Fishing is a total joy. But like any other sport, there are certain rules to abide by. The main one, of course, is just to use some common sense. And if you think all the safety equipment outweighs the fun, cheer up, you could be preparing for a game of American football instead.

CHAPTER TWELVE

The Ghillie, the Hut, the Tales

FISHER: *'Do you think this is the best fly to catch a fish?'*
HIGHLAND GHILLIE: *'Now, if I knew that for certain,
I wouldn't be ghillying.'*

An eccentric, a one-off or simply an ace angler. However you describe a GHILLIE, he remains a unique character and someone who deserves a chapter of his own. This is the man, or woman, (yes, there once was a female ghillie) who's traditionally associated with game fishing.

The dictionary definition is: 'A sportsman's attendant, in the Highlands'. You may come across boatmen and watermen who look after anglers in England and Wales, but the ghillie as such, remains a thoroughly Scottish institution.

Basically, the ghillie is the helper, employed by whoever owns the fishing and his job involves looking after visiting anglers during the fishing season. The rest of the year, his time may be spent on improving pools, repairing paths, or painting huts and boats. Dedicated to the banks and rivers he cares for, when he fishes with you, his brief is a mixed one and can include tackling up, advising on what type of fly to use, taking out wind knots, changing leaders and untangling line. Sometimes, he may have been on the river for 30 years or more and will know every stone and stream of the water for which he cares. So, he'll be able to show you exactly where to wade and cast. And if you're fishing from a boat, he'll usually offer to row. He should know exactly where the fish are lying and be on hand to net that silvery salmon when it takes your fly. He has learned his trade by the water's edge and is one of the greatest asset an angler can possibly have.

From a youngster of 18 on Deeside, to a 70-year-old gentleman on the Border Esk, they come in all ages. Youth has enthusiasm and energy and age, a wealth of patience and knowledge. Both are experiences not to be missed. And ghillies come from all walks of life, from former shepherds to one-time paratroopers. What brings them together is the joy of fishing and a love of the great outdoors. So what makes a good ghillie? Take the words of Willie Donald, he of the royal jumper and someone with more than 40 year's experience of salmon fishing.

'A good ghillie can make a day's fishing, even if it's a blank one; a not so good ghillie can spoil it. In my experience, the former are in the majority and I count some of them as the grandest of my friends. A ghillie's job is just a job, but by no means an easy one. He must know every inch of the water on which he fishes and give of his best to a visiting rod. This is not always easy if conditions are poor, or the visitor is a novice, or a show-off. At the same time, he must remember that the guest's day on the river may be his or her only outing of the year, greatly looked forward to and brought to an end with reluctance.'

In short, if you're offered the services of a ghillie, jump at the chance! And do make sure you make proper use of it. There's nothing worse than a silent fisher who never asks about what sort of fly to use, or where and how to fish a pool. What a waste! Even if it's a blank day, a ghillie can be a great companion, for most are characters and will keep you amused for hours. They are nature's gentlemen and are not only highly knowledgeable about the water and the fish, but may also have a wealth of facts about local plants and wildlife. Mind you, they'll want to know you're taking it seriously and paying attention to the job in hand. Like the Highland chap who tests anglers by letting them fish flyless for several minutes before asking innocently if they've noticed anything wrong. Or the ghillie who likes to liven things up for a fishless and despairing guest. Sensing that his charge, an accountant, is flagging, he creeps up silently behind him and turfs a large rock into the water. Now, of course, the merest hint of a splash is guaranteed to

revive the most despondent fisher, and the man immediately perks up. 'Well, did you hear that?!' says the ghillie. 'A big fish, no doubt about it! If you carry on, I'm sure you'll have him.' And so he leaves his guest to re-double his efforts. Revenge is sweet, though, and sometimes, we fishers do have the last laugh. When the ghillie returns, the accountant is beaming all over his face. 'Guess what', he says. 'I fished that spot, just like you suggested and I caught it!' Amazed, the ghillie watches, as the man opens the car boot to display his catch...a large rock!

As a beginner, it is unlikely you'll come in for such treatment, but the best thing is still to throw yourself at the mercy of the ghillie. If it's any consolation, you must remember that no matter how awful you are, he's usually seen worse. 'I haven't got much fishing experience, but I'm always keen to learn, so tell me when I do something wrong,' always goes down well. Ask for advice and then take it. If he recommends a brown and yellow fly, try it. If it's successful, well and good, but if nothing's happening, then in due course a casual, 'Shall we try this one? It's always been a favourite of mine,' might be in order. A good ghillie will often agree, because a good ghillie wants nothing more than to see you go home with a fish.

Some are more enthusiastic than others, like the former army man who will march you miles up and down the river for hours, calling out instructions on how to cast and where to wade. You can refuse to go on, or burst into tears. Fishing can sometimes be all or nothing and if you haven't fished for a while, a day's casting can leave you feeling pretty sore. So remember, his keenness must really be matched by your's and it is up to the two of you to work it out.

But part of a ghillie's charm will be this enthusiasm, for it's his job to bolster morale. On the first day of a fishing trip, expectations are high and the water is fished hard. But come day three and you've not even seen a tadpole, you may finally turn in desperation to your helper and then it's his responsibility to raise your spirits. Normally the answer goes something like this: 'Aye, the fish will be up soon…' then darkly as an afterthought, '…if they're in the mood, that is.'

For although a ghillie can do a great many things, you must remember that he is not responsible for the weather or the height of the water. In other words, it isn't his fault if you don't take home a salmon. He's not a magician and if the fish aren't there, or they are there but they aren't taking, you can't blame him. If you get really fed up, ask him nicely to fish your rod. As we already know, a beginner can learn an awful lot just by watching. Some ghillies have rather unorthodox ways of casting, but they nearly always catch a salmon, so who cares! And if the does catch a fish, you still get to keep it.

Yes, a witty ghillie will keep you amused for hours;

with tales like that of the young man who arrived to fish with his new bride – a sort of angling honeymoon. Well, he duly fished and she watched adoringly, until at last he hooked a salmon and proudly pulled it into the shallows. At this point, she couldn't stand it any longer and she rushed down the bank, threw her arms around him and accidentally stood on the line, pulling it clean out the fish's mouth. At this point, the ghillie's voice becomes sombre. 'They're divorced now, of course, though I'm not sure that was the main cause.'

But the entertainment's not all one-way and most ghillies appreciate being asked about their family and past jobs, as long as you're not too nosey. The river, you'll find, is a great leveller as there's really only one topic of conversation. A cat may look at a king when fishing, or a ghillie at a lord. Take the story of the man who was helping a foreign prince on his first fishing trip. It proved successful, for after being rowed across the river in a small boat, the royal visitor hooked a salmon. 'Keep your rod tip up, Your Highness,' urged the ghillie, as the man struggled to keep his cool. 'That's good,' soothed the ghillie. 'You're doing just fine. Yes, that's lovely, Your Highness. Now, wind in slowly and remember to keep the tip up. Keep it up! That's right, Your Highness. That's just fine. Now don't let him get behind that rock! Not behind the rock! And keep the tip UP Your Highness! UP! UP! Oh, you great daft bugger! You've lost him!'

Talk like this runs the risk of being carted off to the Tower of London, but the tale goes that the prince was so amused, he insisted that particular ghillie always attended to him on future trips. He also tipped him royally. For although a ghillie is generally paid by whoever owns the beat, it is customary to give him something extra at the end of day. It depends on where you're fishing as to the exact amount, so check with other fishers. It can be anything from five pounds a day and perhaps more if a salmon's caught.

Just how far the comradeship goes is up to both of you, but offers to stay and share lunch are usually politely declined. Most ghillies know what they like and what they don't. An ancient ghillie on the Tay who'd been a prisoner of war in Germany was reminiscing about his time in the camps. 'It wasn't that bad,' he said. 'It was just the food we were given to eat. Pretty dull stuff it was, like dry bread and boiled cabbage. Yes, terribly plain. So I pitied the fellows who'd been used to eating all that fancy food back home. I was all right though,' he continued. 'I'd been brought up in the Highlands and was used to simple things like salmon, grouse and venison.' Quite!

And if you've a ghillie on your beat, the chances are, you'll also have a HUT. This is a small building rather like a garden shed, by the side of the river. It may be bare and basic, but on cold, wet days, it becomes a haven, a place to eat in and shelter from the elements. Most huts are quite basic with just an old wooden table and a bench or two. Others come with all mod cons like lighting and heating. Some are definitely over the top, like the ones with telephone, fax and dishwasher. As a guest, you must treat a hut with respect and leave it tidy for the next lot. The ghillie will usually help, though some are more house-proud than others, like the legendary man from the Spey who lays his table like a five-star dining room, complete with polished glasses, cutlery and napkins.

Whatever it's like, though, a hut is a wonderful way of making fishing a sociable occasion. Here, after the day's efforts, you and your party can unwind and tell huge lies about the ones that got away. As the ghillie said:

'There's two thing I like to see in my water. One's fish and the other's whisky.' Not all fishers drink, but those that do generally catch more fish in the hut than they ever do by the river. Some huts, of course, you enter at your own risk, like the legendary Drammerie on Deeside. You may go

"Honestly, IT WAS!"

in at eight in the evening and still be there eight hours later after an all-night session of singing, drinking and story-telling. Be aware that huts can be places where licensing hours don't apply, and those with a weak constitution should not venture in. For it's on nights like this that tall tales are told. You've heard the old saying, 'How far an angler will stretch the truth depends on how far he can stretch his arms.'

Or the story of the fisher boasting about the size of his latest salmon, 'It must have been five feet at least,' he says. 'Aye', says the ghillie who's listening, 'I've a good story, too. It's about those divers who've been searching the wreckage of a Spanish galleon off the Scottish coast. Do you know the latest? They got down to the seabed to find everything was still there. Nothing had been touched. In fact it was so intact, the ship's lantern was still burning!' 'Nonsense,' replies the fisher. 'The lantern still burning? I don't believe that!' 'Well, I'll tell you what I'll do,' says the ghillie, 'You cut three feet off your fish, and I'll blow out the lantern.'

Or the man who walks into a hut to find three noisy anglers boasting about their salmon, arms outstretched six feet apart. And there in the corner is a wee man with his hands just a foot apart. 'Well now,' says the visitor, 'someone who tells the truth. A salmon twelve inches long, that's more like it.' 'Oh no,' replies the man. 'That was the distance between its eyes!'

And then there are the ones that get away and the

ghillie in Perthshire who regularly helps them to. On desperate, fishless days, he sticks his thermometer into the water and tell his guests, 'You may as well stay in the hut, gentlemen. You'll have to bonk them over the heed, if you want to get them oot today!'

But bad news generally isn't talked about when fishing and sensitive issues are left well alone. They just aren't discussed. No famines, no earthquakes, no political rows, no scandal. No wives leaving husbands: 'We just don't want to spoil a chap's fishing by mentioning it.' No, the only news an angler wants to hear by the water is about the latest feathered fly or lightweight line.

I wish you the luck of the fly-fisher, with screaming reels and tight lines. Those are the rules, but has anyone told the salmon?

GLOSSARY

ANGLING CLUB	Fishing association. Make sure they've got some fly-fishing water!
BACKING	Thin, plaited nylon or heavy monofilament which goes onto the reel before the line. Your backing is the back-up to the line.
BACKING-UP METHOD	Where the fisher starts at the tail of the pool and works upstream. Used when the water is very still and you want to get more movement into your fly.
BARB	The jagged bit on the hook of the fly.
BEAT	A fishing river is divided into stretches of waters called beats.
BLANK	To draw a blank is to catch nothing
BUTT	The handle, often made of cork, on your fly-rod.
CAST or LEADER	The nylon, the link between line and fly.
CASTING	The art of using your rod to throw your line, leader and fly across the water and over the fish.
CLOSE SEASON	The period of time when rivers are not fished, to allow spawning to take place.
COCK	A male salmon.
COVER WATER	To fish over water thoroughly.
DOUBLE	Fly with two-pronged hook.
DRAM	Gaelic for a large tot of whisky. Scotland has around 115 distilleries so there's no excuse!
DROPPER	The second fly attached from the centre of your leader. In theory, it gives two chances of a fish, or even two fish.
FERRULES	The joints of a rod. The rod ferrules slot together to form the long rod.
FIGURE OF EIGHT KNOT	Knot used to join line to leader.
FLY	Feathered hook to attract the fish.
FLY-BOX	A box to keep your flies in.
FLY-TYING	The art of making a fly. Try making you own!

FLY-HOLDER	The small circle of wire above the rod butt to which the fly is attached to stop it flailing about in the wind when not fishing.
FLOG THE WATER	To go at it hammer and tongs for hours.
FLOATING LINE	Line that floats on the water surface. Used more often in summer when levels are lower and water temperatures higher
FOUL HOOK	To hook a fish somewhere other than in its mouth. Foul-hooked fish must be returned to the water.
FRY	The tiny fish that emerges from the salmon egg.
GAFF	Metal hook used to land a fish. Not widely used these days.
GHILLIE	Sportsman's attendant in the Highlands, the helper. Invaluable, entertaining!
GREASING	To grease a knot is to wet it, spit is fine, before you pull it tight. Paradoxically, it stops it from slipping loose again.
GRILSE	A young salmon which has returned to spawn after just one sea winter. Delicious to eat!
HALF-BLOOD KNOT	Common knot to join fly to leader.
HANDLINING	To slowly pull in line as it fishes round in the water. To inject movement into the fly and make it seem more lifelike to the fish.
HEN	A female salmon.
HOOK	Either single, double or treble.
HUT	Often at the side of the beat. Like a garden hut, useful to eat lunch in or shelter in if the weather is really bad.
KELT	A salmon that has spawned and is heading back down river to the sea. Thin and blackened, Kelts are inedible and if caught, should be put back.
LAND A FISH	Bringing the fish to the bank or into the net.
LEADER	Your nylon, the link between line and fly (See also CAST)
LIE	Good place to fish over, as salmon like to find a good lie in the river.
LIFE JACKET	Possible life saver. Wear a proper angling one if the water looks dodgy!
LINE	Your line is the next thing on your reel after the backing and it's the line that takes leader and fly out across the water.

MITTENS	Gloves cut off at the joints, useful to feel the line, yet still keep hands warm.
NET	For salmon. A large, unwieldy object, useful for getting the fish from the water to the bank.
NYLON	The link between line and fly, often known as a cast or leader.
OVERHEAD CAST	A standard cast when fly-fishing. Take the rod back and then arc it forward, allowing the line to come shooting out down the rod.
PARR	A young salmon, a little fish of between three and five inches.
PERMIT	Either written or verbal, everyone needs a permit to fish.
PLAY A FISH	The term given to the battle between the angler and the fish once he's on the hook. It means giving him line when he tries to run and reeling him in when he tires.
POACHING	Definitely not allowed! Fishing without permission, or using illegal methods.
POOL	The river is divided into pools and fish rest in pools before heading upstream again. A good place to fish over.
PRIEST	The heavy, blunt instrument like a small truncheon used to kill the fish, when you catch it.
PULL	When the fish takes your fly and then spits it out, you have 'had a pull'... There's some momentary excitement and at least you know there's something in the river!
REEL	The contraption your backing and line goes onto and which sits on the rod. You wind in your reel to pull in a fish.
REEL SEAT	Where your reel sits when it's attached to the rod.
RINGS	The wire guides on the rod through which the line is threaded.
ROD	The long, stick like instrument used to throw your line across the water.
ROD LICENCE	Needed in England, Wales and Northern Ireland, though not in Scotland.
RUN	Salmon are on a run when returning upriver to spawn.
SHOOT LINE	To use your rod to send line shooting through the rings on the rod and across the water.

SINKING LINE	Line that sinks in the water to take the fly down to the fish. Used in cold weather and when levels are high.
SLEEVE	The cover for your rod, made of fabric, plastic or metal. Some expensive ones are made of leather.
SPEY CAST	Forward, rather than backward cast. Useful in the wind or where there are bushes or trees behind you.
STRIKE	To strike. What you must do when you think there's a fish on the end of your line, bring the rod tip up quickly and smoothly, to try to hook the fish securely.
TACKLE	Your fishing equipment.
TACKLE SHOP	Where you buy your fishing equipment.
TACKLE BAG	What you put your tackle in, e.g. reel, flies, etc.
TAILER	Old-fashioned metal instrument used to land a fish by looping it around its tail.
TENANT	The person who rents the fishing.
TIMESHARE	Where you buy fishing for a certain amount of time each year, for a fixed term of several years or in perpetuity .
TIP RING	The final wire eye on the tip of your rod.
TO MEND LINE	To take out an upstream or downstream curve in the line, or to hold back or accelerate the passage of the line and thus the fly. Do this by swinging the rod tip and the line should follow.
TOUCH A FISH	When a fish nibbles at your fly, you have touched a fish.
TREBLE	Fly with three-pronged hook.
TUBE FLY	Fly where the body comes separate from the hook. Useful if you break a barb, you just replace the hook, not the whole thing.
WADDINGTON	A type of fly.
WADERS	Extended wellies. Essential for staying dry when wading. Thigh waders come to the thigh, chest waders to the chest.
WADING STICK	Stick made out of wood or metal, weighted at the end, to help you move more steadily in the water.
WIND KNOTS	Tiny knots that appear in the nylon as it flails about in the wind and snap it when a fish is hooked. A common complaint for the beginner!